Boxing: The American Martial Art

Boxing: The American Martial Art

a 12 week boxing course

R. Michael Onello

Turtle Press   Hartford

To contact the author or to order additional copies of this book:

Turtle Press
P.O. Box 290206
Wethersfield, CT 06129-0206
1-800-778-8785
www.turtlepress.com

ISBN 1-880336-82-0
LCCN 2003017185

Printed in the United States of America

10 9 8 7 6 5 4 3 2 1

Library of Congress Cataloging-in-Publication Data

Onello, Robert M.
  Boxing : the American martial art : a 12 week boxing course / Robert M. Onello.— 1st ed.
     p. cm.
  ISBN 1-880336-82-0
  1. Boxing—Training. I. Title.

GV1137.6 .O64 2003
796.83—dc22

                              2003017185

This book is dedicated to my beautiful daughter Lauren. I hope this writing inspires you on to greatness in whatever you set out to achieve. You certainly have been my inspiration, Thank you Lauren!

Boxing: The American Martial Art

Contents

Why this Book?

There are certainly enough books on boxing out there. This may be true, but they get caught up in the author's accomplishments or tell a story on the history of a certain aspect of boxing. And most are as unknowledgeable and out dated as the U.S. Recommended Daily Amount and the food pyramid. There are very few publications that have dealt with the specifics of boxing and training in a day to day curriculum format. No one wants to take responsibility and say, "Follow this exactly for three months. It works!" All they do is give you information and you have to put it together on your own. If it fails, it's your own doing.

The purpose of this text is to educate those people in organized boxing, as well as boxers and the common individual, to get into the best mental and physical shape of their lives.

As a former amateur boxer and currently a licensed professional boxing coach / trainer who trains amateur and pro-fighters, holds local boxing clinics and teaches box-aerobics classes at health clubs nationally, it amazes me how <u>inadequately</u> most boxers train.

This Book is About . . .

A diversified pool of training techniques and a method of instruction used by the world's best-conditioned athletes, set up in a curriculum format that breaks down the process and educates you step by step. Being in a strong, solid and sound training program, it will teach as well as train you, regardless of your entry fitness level. Great emphasis is placed on the pre-conditioning that is needed to box as well as the fundamental skills that will be required and acquired. This book is like having a personal trainer and a boxing instructor with you at your location. Your questions will be answered: How long do I train? How often? What exercises work specific areas? What drills and when to do them?

Consider This:

The reality is active people live fuller lives with more stamina, resist illness, stay trim and are less stressed. Boxing is the hottest work-out to fight the two most dangerous opponents: stress and physical inactivity. Why box? Some of the benefits include speed, upper and lower body strength, coordination, self-defense, cardiovascular endurance and stamina, improved mental and physical health, and self-confidence.

Having a plan is half the battle. This book is that plan! Your part is to make the commitment to consistently train 2 to 3 days per week, for about one hour. The benefits will amaze you. Your confidence level will soar, and your muscles will tighten, tone and strengthen. I wish you success!

I Wish You Success!

My current student, Kenny Blair affirms the proof of these prin-ciples. In less then two years of training under my direction, he has already won several U.S.A. Boxing/sanctioned Florida amateur-tournaments and is the current 147 lb. Southeastern JR. Olympic-Champion. He spars regularly with national amateur champions. Blair has also sparred at world Heavyweight champion Lennox Lewis' training camp in Poconos, PA; three weeks before the Lewis-Tyson fight in June 2002. Blair went two competitive rounds with Lewis' trainer Emanuel Steward's world ranked featherweight Sugar Rey Beltran. Based on his outstanding performance, Blair and I were invited back to Lewis' next training camp.

How to Use This Book

- The word "coach" and "instructor" are used interchangeably throughout this book.

- The word "boxer" and "student" are also used interchangeably throughout this book.

- "Student" can be male or female. No bias is intended by the terms his / her or him / her.

- It is strongly recommended by the author that prior to starting this program the student have a medical check-up by a licensed medical practitioner.

- Training duration: Two days per week. (Additional days can be added at any time). Sessions will last for a period of 1 to 2 hours.

- Use the glossary and equipment lists as references throughout the book when needed.

- Pre-lessons/training-conditioning (Lessons A, B, C, D, E and F) are to be performed prior to the Lessons 1-25. They are broken down systematically and continually change to make sure every muscle group is targeted once or twice a week, with careful attention to not overworking the muscles, including the heart.

- Each numbered lesson represents a workout day.

- It is important to follow the workout in precise order, because each boxing lesson systematically accompanies a pre-lesson/training-conditioning lesson. The curriculum was designed to stretch and strengthen as well as build endurance while acquiring boxing skills.

- A "punch number system" is included for memorizing punches and calling them out loud rapidly.

- Look to the upper-left corner of each Lesson, beginning with Lesson 1 under the title (heading). There you will find your instructions (guide) for the lesson.

Equipment Guide

Protective Gear:

Full protective gear consists of the following: mouthpiece, foul protector, headgear, hand-wraps, and boxing gloves.

B/g: Boxing bag gloves. Worn to protect the hands during practice

Boxing gloves. Worn to protect the hands during sparring.

Foul protector: Cup worn over the groin area.

Headgear: Padded "helmet" is worn over the head to protect the head and face.

H/w: Hands wrapped with protective cotton wrapping.

M/p: Mouthpiece worn to help prevent mouth injuries and knockouts.

Training Equipment:

Double end bag: A round air filled bag resembling a soccer ball, held in place in mid-air between two rubber straps, one at each end of the bag.

Focus pads: A catcher's mitt type pad worn by a coach or trainer to receive/deflect blows.

Heavy-bag: Canvas or leather oblong shaped bag which hangs from the ceiling.

Speed bag: Small bag, resembling a papaya, hanging on a ceiling platform. You strike rapidly in succession, creating a consistent rhythm.sion, creating a consistent rhythm.

Maize ball: Weighted bag (the size and shape of a "swollen pear") hanging from a cord at chin height. Used for the purpose of head movement and reflexes as it swings at you, you move your head out of the way.

Uppercut bag: Canvas or leather oblong shaped bag hanging horizontally at waist height.

Conditioning

Chapter One

In this Chapter:

Introduction to Stretching

Introduction to Abdominal & Oblique Exercises

Introduction to Hyperextensions

Introduction to Cardiovascular Endurance Strength Training

Introduction to Strength and Muscle Training

Strength and Muscle Training Combined with Cardiovascular Training

Equipment list:

Ab-rocker
Ankle-weights
Bench
Chin-up bar
Cone
Dip bar
Dumbbell's
Jump –rope
Mouthpiece

Plyometric ball
Plyometric box
Push-up handles
Roman-chair
Stick
Stopwatch
Towel
Weighted head strap
Wheel roller

Introduction to Stretching

Stretching can benefit anything you do by reducing tension and making you limber; it increases coordination by giving you flexibility with added range of motion. Stretching is great as a pre-workout activity to loosen up by getting the blood flowing. This promotes good circulation so you can perform at your optimal level and prevent injury. You can also benefit from stretching as a post workout activity to revitalize you while you slow and cool down the body, thereby preventing soreness.

During a boxing match, expect to find yourself in many awkward positions. The boxer who is more agile and able to punch from multiple angles will prevail.

When you finish stretching, try drinking a glass of fresh water to flush toxins from your system. Water allows your body to loosen up while lubricating your joints. It is my opinion that stretching will give you a toned, cut-up look.

Stretching can be done anywhere or anytime. It feels fantastic!

STRETCHING: Standing Stretches

LESSON A to be completed every workout.

Stretch until you feel a good easy stretch with a light burning sensation. Never bounce or stretch to the point of pain. Hold the stretch for at least five seconds.

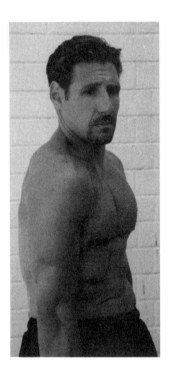

Shoulder Point – Stand relaxed with your feet shoulder width apart and your arms hanging down at your sides. Push one shoulder forward and out. Try to keep the other shoulder straight, not moving backward.

Area loosened: shoulders / pectorals / trapezoids / upper-back

Shake- Shake out arms and legs.

Area loosened: arms / legs

Knee -Circle – Stand with your ankles inner thighs and knees all touching, keeping your feet together. Slightly bend at the waist with your hands on your knees. Make small circles in each direction.

Area loosened: ankle / knees

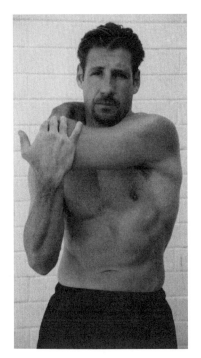 

<u>One Arm Stretches</u> – Pull your elbow across your chest. Then raise your elbow above your head and push it down gently.

Area loosened: shoulders / upper –back / triceps

Finger Interlace – Place your arms straight out in front of you. Interlace your fingers at shoulder height with palms facing you. Push your hands forward. Repeat this process by flipping your hands so your knuckles are towards you and continue to push out in front of you. Repeat the entire process with your hands held straight out above your head.

Area loosened: shoulders / upper-back / arms / hands / fingers / wrists

<u>Elbow Side Bend</u> – With arms held over your head, create a box. Pull your left elbow with your right hand and bend to the right side. Pull your right elbow with your left hand and bend to the left side.

Area loosened: shoulder / upper-back / arms

<u>Arm Circles </u>– Make circles with both arms forward and backward like a windmill. In addition, try performing this movement with one arm at a time.

Area loosened: shoulders / arms / upper-back

<u>Straight Arm Circles </u>– Hold your arms straight out at your sides pointing your fingers. Make small circles forward and backward.

Area loosened: shoulders

Wall Push – Facing a wall or immovable object place one foot forward and the other back behind you with your feet pointing straight to the front of you and your shoulders square. Place your palms to the wall, pushing slightly.

Area loosened: calf / hamstrings / quadriceps.

<u>Mouth Stretch</u> – Open and close your mouth very wide. Move your jaw from side to side. Extend your lower jawbone out and in. Close your mouth and bite down with slight pressure.

Area loosened: mouth / jaw

<u>Calf Stretches</u> – Stand with your feet shoulder width apart and flat to the floor. Raise your heels up off the surface and then lower back down to the surface. For your second set, remain in the up position on the balls of your feet so you have constant resistance. Proceed as with the latter.

Area loosened: calf

<u>Knee to Shoulder</u> – Stand with your feet at shoulder width. Rapidly raise each knee individually to your chest.

Area loosened: outside hip / buttocks

<u>Foot to Buttocks</u> – From behind, pull each ankle one at a time up toward your shoulder, going straight up slowly and trying not to bend forward.

Area loosened: quads / knees

<u>One Leg Up</u> – Place the back of your heel on a solid surface, waist high, so your leg is straight out in front of you. Bend forward at the waist touching your extended foot with each hand. Repeat this with both hands at the same time.

Area loosened: hamstrings

Squat – Stand with your feet shoulder width apart. Squat down to touch the floor with the palms of your hands, keeping both feet flat to the floor with your toes pointed forward.

Area loosened: knees / back / ankles / Achilles tendon / groin / front lower leg

Palm to Palm Box – Form a box with your arms, elbows pointing outward at shoulder level. Hands together palm to palm, bend and push your fingers from left to right.

Area loosened: hands / wrist

 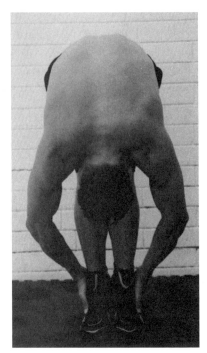

<u>Waist Bends</u> - Stand with your feet shoulder width apart, bending at the waist. Touch the floor with your palms. Repeat the motion, only this time bring your legs together.

Area loosened: hamstrings

<u>Back Bend</u> – Stand with your feet at shoulder width, hands supporting your lower back. Bend backwards as far as you can.

Area loosened: back / Abs

Neck Movements – Stand with your feet shoulder width apart. Bend your neck from side to side, touching your ear to your shoulder. Then proceed to make circles rolling your head and neck to the left then right. Next make your chin touch your chest, then drop your head as far back as you can.

Area loosened: neck / traps

Arm Crosses – Stand with your feet shoulder width apart and your arms crossed over your chest. Proceed to look over your shoulder, pointing your chin in the direction you are looking. Alternate sides.

Area loosened: neck

 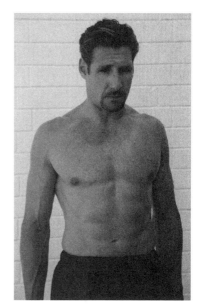

<u>Shoulders</u> – Stand with your feet shoulder width apart, keeping your arms in close to your body. Proceed to pull your shoulders up and down, then make circles forward and backward, first with one arm, then both arms at the same time.

Area loosened: shoulders

STRETCHING: Floor Stretches

<u>Butterfly</u> – Sit with your legs open and the soles of your feet touching one another. Grasp your feet with your hands, letting your elbows rest on your knees and thighs, pressing down slightly.

Area loosened: groin

<u>Foot Stretches</u> – Rotate each foot in a circle, then pull up and push down on each foot.

Area loosened: feet / ankles / heel / toes / Achilles tendon / arch

<u>Superman</u> – Lying on your stomach raise your head, legs and arms as if you were skydiving or being pulled up by strings.

Area loosened; back / neck / chest / hamstrings

<u>Tee Stretch</u> – Sit with one leg straight out in front, the other bent at the knee with its sole resting against your thigh. Gently lean forward. Touch each hand to your extended foot, then bring both hands at the same time to your foot. For an additional stretch, while the hand on the same side as the extended leg is touching the foot, touch your opposite elbow and forearm to the floor.

Area loosened: hamstring / calf

<u>Straight Leg Stretch</u> – Sitting with both legs straight out, lean forward from the waist, extending your arms to touch your toes.

Area loosened: hamstrings

36

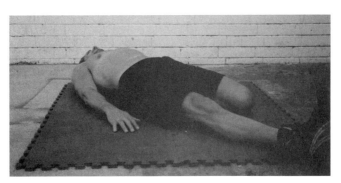

Leg to the Side Stretch – Sit with one leg out in front of you, the other leg back and to the side of you. Reach out and touch your toes in front of you with each hand. Then touch the floor in front of you with both hands at the same time. Lay back so your back is flat to the floor, keeping your knee down to the floor the entire time.

Area loosened: calf / hamstrings

<u>Lying Knee to Chest</u> – Lying on the floor with one leg extended out in front of you, bend and pull the other leg into your chest.

Area loosened: hamstrings / knee

<u>Legs Over Head</u> – Lying on your back, roll your legs directly over your body so that you are resting on your shoulders and neck. Have your toes touch the floor above your head.

Area loosened; back / buttocks / hamstrings

<u>Rack</u> - Lie on your back with your legs straight out in front of you and elevated slightly off the ground and your arms slightly elevated pointed straight out overhead. Reach with your fingers and toes as if you were being pulled from each direction top and bottom. This is an elongation stretch.

Area loosened: Abs / oblique

<u>Bow Stretch</u> – Kneel down on the floor with your knees touching each other, your chin tucked and your buttocks down. Bend forward at the waist keeping your hips back and trying to touch the floor with your chest. Keep your arms extended forward and your fingers pointed.

Area loosened: triceps / latissimus-dorsi / Abs

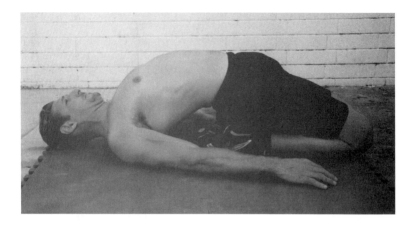

Reverse Bow – Kneeling down on the floor with your knees touching each other, bend backward keeping your knees down and together. Try to rest the back of your head and shoulders on the floor.

Area loosened: quads / ankles

Neck Pull – Lying on your back, bend your knees and rest the soles of your feet on the floor. Interlace your fingers behind your head. Gently pull the back of your neck so your chin touches your chest.

Area loosened: neck / spine

<u>Reverse Bridge</u> – Get down on your palms and knees, keeping your fingers pointed back toward your knees. Lean back slightly.

Area loosened: wrist / forearm

<u>Kneeling Bent Leg Forward</u> – From a kneeling position, place one leg out in front of you. Keeping the sole of your foot down, slide the other leg behind you resting it on your knee and shin. Try to touch the floor with your fingertips by pulling down with your shoulders, being careful not to lean forward.

Area loosened: groin / shoulder / quads / hamstrings

41

Spinal Twist – While sitting, place one leg out in front of you. Cross over it with the other, keeping the sole of that foot flat to the floor and up against the outside of the straight leg. Bend the elbow of the arm that is on the opposite side of the straight leg, placing it on the inside of the crossed leg and pushing it slightly. Put your opposite arm out behind you for balance and try to look over your shoulder while rotating your body. Repeat on the opposite side.

Area loosened: spine / lower-back / hips

<u>Knee to Floor</u> – Lying on your back with your hands interlaced behind your head, bend your knees and cross one leg over the other, keeping the sole of your bent leg flat to the floor. Push gently on the top crossed leg so the pressure causes the bottom bent leg's knee to touch the floor. Keep your waist parallel to the floor and your shoulders neck and elbows pinned to the floor.

Area loosened: lower-back /sides / hips

43

Introduction to Abdominal & Oblique Exercises

A boxer must have a strong firm abdomen because everything emanates from here. According to martial arts theory, your abdomen is your center. Just below your navel is your core where your chi is stored. From the air you draw upon, your breath is converted to energy. The Chinese believe all life begins in your chi.

Related to boxing, the abdomen must be able to defend a body attack. If your defense fails, you have to absorb body blows. Your abdomen will become your outer armor, especially for the rib cage and kidney area.

Additionally, having a strong midsection increases your punching power with added support for your back. From an opponent's perspective, it is very "intimidating" to see a cut up lean abdomen. It relays a message that you have trained very hard and are in great cardiovascular shape, ready to go the distance.

Abs

LESSON B to be completed each workout.

Choose and perform two of the following exercises. Perform exercise from start to failure. Try to increase with each week, until you are at a comfortable level.

Roman Chair Sit Up – Perform in three parts:

1. Extend yourself fully so your head almost touches the floor. Cross your arms over your chest.

2. Keeping your hands in the same position, resist gravity by stopping at the halfway point, staying level in mid air.

3. Proceed as in part 1 except, stop at a 45-degree angle, which is about quarter of the motion. This will keep constant pressure on your abdominal section. Upon conclusion, hold your body at a level position in mid air for as long as you can without moving, resisting the downward pull of gravity.

Crunch with Bench – Perform in four parts:

1. Lying with your back to the floor and your legs over a bench so your calves are resting on the bench, place your hands on the back of your head, not interlaced. Proceed to crunch upward.

2. Place your hands crossed over your chest and perform crunches.

3. Place your fingertips on your temples and perform crunches.

4. Place your fingertips just below navel and perform crunches.

For the finish hold your abdomen with constant pressure in a tight squeeze elevated above the floor (with your fingertips in any one of the positions), for as long a period as you can.

<u>Finger to Toe</u> – Lying down with your back to the floor, extend your legs and arms parallel, keeping them slightly off the floor. Raise them simultaneously, meeting above your centerline (mid-navel). Gently raise your shoulders and head off the floor as well.

<u>Ab Rocker</u> - Crunch forward bringing your head and shoulders off the floor, trying not to use the muscles in your arms. At your halfway mark through the set, incorporate your feet in the movement bringing your knees to your chest at the same time your head and shoulders come up off the floor. Try to keep your toes pointed throughout the movement.

<u>Wheel Roller</u> – Kneel on your knees. Keep your head up, looking forward, while keeping your feet off the floor behind you. Roll to the left, the center, then to the right.

Boxer's Sit Up – Perform in three parts:

1. Lying down with your back to the floor, keep your legs straight out in front of you off the floor and place your hands behind your head. Bend your knees one at a time, pulling them toward your upper body as you bring your shoulders and head to meet your incoming legs. All body parts move at the same time to your centerline, contracting and expanding.

2. Perform in the same manner as part 1 except bring one leg in at a time, while the other remains straight out, elevated above the floor.

3. Perform in the same manner as part 1, but as you are contracting up to your centerline slightly twist at the side of your waist, bringing your left elbow to your right knee then the right elbow to the left knee.

Boxer's Sit Up # 2 – To be performed at the finish of the boxer's sit up. Place your hands palm side down under your buttocks, keeping your head off the floor. Hold your legs straight out in front of you, about five inches off the floor for a period of time, then raise your legs about three feet off the floor and hold for a period of time. Repeat the exercise, except open and close your legs like a scissors at both elevations.

Diamond Sit Up – Lie on your back, with the soles of your feet pressing against each other and the outer parts of your knees close to the floor. Hands are over your head close to the floor. Grab and hold one of your thumbs, so that your elbows point outward like your knees. Raise your head, shoulders and chest in a forward and upward motion off the floor. Your fingers should now point towards your toes.

<u>Straps</u> - Put your arms through the straps so they are under your armpits, do not support your weight with your hands. Perform in five parts with a rest period in between:

1. Bring your knees to your chest, extend your legs forward, and lower them slowly.

2. Bring your knees to your chest keeping them bent the entire time. Try to keep your feet close to your buttocks. Another variation would be to bring your knees to your chest as in the latter except upon lowering them, straighten your legs, bringing your feet close to the floor.

3. Keeping your legs straight, lift them out in front of you.

4. Hold your legs together straight out in front of you for as long as you can.

5. Bring your knees to your chest and hold there for as long as you can. Lower so they are level with your waist and continue to hold.

Obliques

Choose and perform one of the following exercises. Perform exercises from start to failure. Try to increase with each week, until you are at a comfortable level.

Weighted Twist – Perform in four parts, standing with your feet shoulder width apart and firm to the floor. Hold a weighted plate vertically in front of you, with your elbows in close to your body just below your navel.

1. Simply twist from the waist up, making sure your shoulder points out in front of your chin on each turn.

2. Flip the weight and hold it flat. Now twist at a rapid pace.

3. Extend the weight further out in front of you so that during the twisting motion the weight will be brought behind your back.

4. Hold the weight out in front of you at chest level, never lowering your arms during the motion.

Weighted Side Bends - Standing with feet shoulder width apart and firm to the floor. Hold hand weights at your sides. Simply bend at the waist only, to one side and then the other. For the first half of the set try to bring the weight down your leg to your knees. During the second half perform more rapidly not going as far down with the weight. At the conclusion, hold the weight next to your shoulders, palms facing out in front of you with your elbows pointed down.

Roman Chair - Get into the chair sideways with your legs crossed over one another under the bar and your hands interlaced behind your head. Proceed to go down sideways, twisting when you get to the bottom so you are looking at the floor. When you get back up, try to look over your shoulder. This exercise can also be done without the twist.

Stick Twist - Stand with your feet shoulder width apart and firm to the ground. Have the stick behind you, resting on your shoulders and traps. Place your hands on the ends of the stick (hands can be placed closer together on the stick, to work different areas of the abdomen.) Proceed to twist from the waist up.

Variations:

A. Bend over at the waist so your elbows point to the ground when out in front of you.

B. Twist with a slight dipping motion when your elbow is out in front of you. Finish with the stick pointing up to the ceiling.

C. Bend from side to side as opposed to twisting.

Introduction to Hyperextensions

Lesson C. Perform every other class on a roman chair (also referred to as a hyperextension bench).

 In the sport of boxing there are many movements that require strong back muscles and agility, such as bending, bobbing and weaving. Therefore a boxer must have a strong back. All the body parts are connected through the back for boxing purposes. This explains why <u>fifty</u> <u>percent of your power comes from your back,</u> and when you take a shot to the head it is absorbed throughout your upper back.

Results from this exercise can benefit the internal as well as the external oblique muscles of the abdomen. Not only does this exercise build strength and muscle, it is also a great stretch.

Mechanics:

1. Hands are placed behind your head with your fingers interlaced.
2. Proceed to lower yourself down to the floor, then raise yourself back to a level position.
3. Do one set to failure.

Area worked: Primarily lower back / Upper back, including Traps / Hamstrings / Abdominal area.

Introduction to Cardiovascular Endurance Strength Training

Oxygen is everywhere, yet in the ring the boxer will seemingly never have enough.

The heart is a muscle that has to work constantly, even at rest, so it has to be stronger then any other muscle; it is that simple. The cardiovascular system supplies blood to tissues in the body at all times. During strenuous physical activities like boxing, the large muscles require almost twenty times more oxygen then their normal resting metabolic rate, which means the heart has to pump more, while simultaneously removing the extra waste by-products. "That's a lot of work!"

It makes good sense for a boxer to strengthen the heart. The fastest results in the entire program can be obtained through cardiovascular training. It is the foundation for boxing, which enriches the whole program.

The following routines were designed for the purpose of acquiring hand, foot, and eye coordination. This will teach you to use each individual body part as a whole unit and most importantly, it will give you endurance (the latter will increase your breathing capability in the ring). With increased breathing capability, you will have clearer and faster thought processes and faster reaction time.

LESSON D. Perform twice a week at the start or end of the lesson. Choose one of the following exercises. In addition, for the third day of cardiovascular training, go for a long run consisting of running forward, backward and sideways. Over a few months period build up to a duration of 45-60 minutes. Wearing a mouthpiece is optional, but I do recommend getting used to breathing with it!

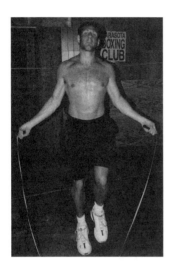 

Jump Rope – Keep your legs close together with your arms hanging down close to your sides and your head looking forward. Start to jump with the rope behind you, having it come forward overhead using your wrists only. Try to stay on the balls of your feet, not bending your legs. Jump for three rounds of three minutes each, with a one-minute break in between. Prior to a competition you can increase the number of rounds.

Variation: Jump in rhythms such as twice on one leg, twice on the other leg or once on one leg, twice on the other or ten jumps on one leg, ten jumps on the other leg. Try performing jumping jacks with your legs as you're jumping rope. Try running forward and backward or running in place (with the latter, start with your knees low at first then bring them up as high as your chest level) as you are jumping. The combinations are endless. Experiment with them!

Sprints - Perform in seven parts:

1. Set two cones approximately thirty feet apart. Sprint from cone to the other, using the walk back as a rest period. Complete four sets.

2. Same as the previous set except running backwards.

3. Same as the previous set except running sideways. Be extra careful not to cross your legs.

4. Sprint from one cone to the other, touch the ground and sprint back immediately in one continuous run.

5. Same as the previous set except repeat two consecutive times.

6. Set six cones ten feet apart from one another. Run to each cone stopping at each then instantly starting to run to the next cone.

7. Place two cones sixty feet apart. Sprint from cone to the other, using the walk back as a rest period.

Advanced variation to the long run (prior to competition) : Run at your normal pace, then sprint 20 to 50 yards, depending on your level of conditioning. Continue running at your normal pace until your heart rate levels off. Keep repeating this pattern for the entire length of the run.

Plyometric Drills

Nothing can raise the level of performance faster then plyometrics. They are designed to teach the muscles to reach maximum strength and speed, which will produce explosive power and agility in a very short period of time.

By strengthening all three muscle contractions, eccentric (lengthening), isometric (stopping) and concentric (shortening), it makes you a multidirectional athlete with coordinated footwork.

Specifically designed for boxing, in my program I tend to lean towards aerobic plyometric drills. They were traditionally designed to be anaerobic. You can experiment both ways, with rest periods and without. I encourage you to get creative and invent your own drills.

Here are samples of a few drills that have worked for me:

Time each drill with a stopwatch. Perform for as many seconds as possible with the goal being a maximum of a full three-minute round, for a total of six drills. Keep in mind each drill is performed as rapidly as possible.

Calf Jump - Stand on the balls of your feet, not bending your legs. Proceed to jump up as high as you can off the floor consecutively with as much hang time as possible. Incorporate your arms for added power and height.

Squat Jump – Squat with your feet shoulder width apart and your hands at your sides behind you. Propel yourself off the floor as high as you can, bringing your knees to your chest. Another variation is a standing jump: same format applies except your start position is standing.

Box Jump - Stand in front of a plyometric box (made of wood or plastic, ranging in height from 6 to 24 inches, top-landing surface is 18 to 24 inches) and proceed to jump onto it. Try to land in the middle of the box. As soon as you land jump backwards off it. Keep in mind as soon as you land, you must jump. No double jumps.

Cone Hop - Stand next to a cone. Hop over it from side to side, making sure your knees come up as high as you can. Your feet must clear the cone. Land and jump. No double jumps. Hit the floor and explode back off of it.

Multiple Box Jump - Stand next to the box sideways. Jump up on the box, land, then jump off the box to the other side, land, then repeat, from the other side back up onto the box. No double jumps. You must land and jump in one motion.

Jump from Box - Stand in the middle of the box in the same position as a standing jump. Proceed to jump off the box as high and far as you can. As soon as you make contact with the floor, immediately jump straight up, bringing your knees to your chest.

Side to Side Hop - Place two cones about three feet apart. Hop with your feet together between the cones. For a variation of this exercise try standing on one leg. Finish the set then alternate legs.

Introduction to Strength and Muscle Training

In the sport of boxing you must have a lean strong body, capable of generating tremendous speed which will produce power.

Performing the following routine along together with working the bags will develop your muscles in proportion to your body "the way it was naturally meant to be developed," the same as our forefathers, who worked everything by hand without electric power tools, engines or machines doing the work for them.

As a boxer you do not want to have big bulging overdeveloped muscles. Carrying the extra muscle would only tire and slow you down.

The following exercises are designed to let your body develop into its natural shape and size allowing you to reach your "maximum potential strength" naturally. In addition to becoming a fine-tuned athlete, a boxer must train two very important areas of the body beyond what the average athlete trains. The first area is the neck. This will help you to absorb and maneuver away from punches quickly. The second are the hands. Remember a boxer is only as strong as his hands, "the point of impact" where everything meets.

The leg routine is designed to build coordination, muscle, stamina, strength, flexibility and speed without putting on much muscle size.

LESSON E. Proper breathing will maximize your ability to perform well. Monitor your breath. Inhale on the down stroke, exhale on the up and pull stroke. All exercises are performed to failure for one set (until you cannot do anymore).

Push-Up – Lying on your stomach, raise up onto your hands and toes. Keep your back straight and your head up, looking forward. Lower yourself back down to the floor. Do half the set with your elbows pointed out and the remaining half with your elbows pointed back in close to your body.

Inverted Push-Up - The same as a regular push-up except your feet are elevated above the floor.

Diamond Push-Up – The same as a regular push-up except form a triangle with your hands out in front of you with your elbows pointed out. Perform in three parts:

1. Hands are as far forward as possible out in front of your head.
2. Hands are between your chest and navel.
3. Hands are below your navel.

Handle Push-Up - The same as a regular push-up except using handles. Perform in two parts:

1. The handles are placed horizontal. (Elbows pointed out)

2. The handles are placed vertical. (Elbows pointed back)

Incline / Decline push-up – The same as a regular push-up except using steps. Put your hands or feet on the third step from the floor. Start the exercise with your elbows pointed out, while finishing with your elbows pointed back. This will enable your hands to be under your navel.

Dips – Place two chairs shoulder width apart. Get between them and place one hand on each. Bend your knees so you're not touching the ground. Your hands will be holding you up. Proceed to lower yourself, then rise back up again. Keep your head up and looking forward. Note: this exercise can also be done with a dip bar.

Reverse bench dips - With your back to the bench and your legs straight out in front of you on your heels, place your arms behind you so your elbows point backward and your hands are palms down on the edge of the bench. Proceed to lower and raise yourself.

Pull-ups - Using a bar, pull yourself up, then lower yourself down. With your palms facing you, fully extended your arms; try not to rock back and forth. The last few reps of the set, keep constant tension on your biceps by not fully extending your arms. Only lower yourself half to a quarter of the way down. Try to keep your knees bent and feet crossed.

Chin-ups - Position yourself as in a pull-up but with your palms facing out away from you. Do one rep with bar in front of you and the other with it behind your neck (alternating).

Dumbbells are to be used at whatever weight feels comfortable. Perform one set of 10-15 reps.

Biceps Curl - Alternate days between standing, sitting, incline and flat. Hold the weights horizontally at your sides and raise your hands up one at a time. Halfway through the set switch to a hammer curl, by bringing your hands up vertically (thumbs up). Variation: you can rotate your hands by starting vertically and finishing horizontally.

Choose one of the following three; alternate each workout:

Kickbacks - Place your right knee on a flat bench and your left foot on the floor. Bend forward. Keep your head up while your back and shoulders are level. Your left arm is in front of you for support. Your right hand is holding the weight vertically, in close and tight to your body. Raise the weight backward so it is level with your back; hold it there for a few seconds, then lower it.

Overhead Pullover - Standing or sitting, raise your arms above your head and form a triangle with your hands. Hold the bar vertical in the middle of your hands over your head. Try to keep your elbows pointed forward. Lower your forearms then extend them back up again.

French Curl - Sitting or standing, put your left hand behind your head, with your right hand supporting your elbow. Hold the weight vertically. Turn your forearm so it rests on your head and the weight is over the right shoulder.

Choose one of the following four; alternate each workout:

Flat Bench Press - Lie with your back on the bench, feet on floor and your head down. Hold the weights horizontally to each side of you. Press the weights up, and then slowly let them come back down.

Incline Press - Same as above, except the bench is set at an incline.

Decline Press - Same as above, except the bench is set at a decline.

Flies - Same as any angle from above but hold the weight out at your sides and slightly bend arms with your palms facing up. Raise the weights and flex your chest when the weights are directly over it.

Pullovers - Lie across the short part of the bench with your feet firm to floor and your hands up over behind you, forming a dia-mond with the weight in the middle vertically. Lower the weight down to the floor, and then raise it back up over your chest.

One Arm Bent-Over Rows - Bend over at the waist, with your right knee on the bench and your right hand on the bench for support. Your left foot is firm to the floor, your head is up, and the weight is vertical in your left hand. Pull it up as high as you can, almost to your lat. Lower it back down to the floor slowly. (A full stretch is required.) Variation: You can start with the weight horizontal, turning it vertical on the way up. Do this by rotating your wrist.

Choose one of the following two; alternate each workout.

Shoulder Press - Sitting or standing, keep your head forward with the weights held horizontally in each hand at shoulder level and your elbows pointed outward. Press the weights upward, one side at a time.

Lateral Raises - Stand with your feet shoulder width apart.

Side: Weights are held at your side vertically. Using both arms at the same time, raise the weights up and out to shoulder level, hold them there for five seconds and then lower them.

Front: Hold the weights in front of your legs horizontally, lift them straight out at the same time to your chest level. Hold them there for five seconds then lower them.

Curved: With the weights in front of you vertically, lean forward with your head up, lift them out and up over your shoulders, so that your elbows are pointed up. Throughout this exercise it should feel as if strings were tied to your elbows, with balloons at the other end to raising your arms up to the sky.

STRENGTH TRAINING: Legs

Lunges - Stand and hold the weights vertical at your sides with your feet shoulder width apart. Take a step forward with the left foot, slightly outside your shoulder width stance. Bring your right knee almost to the floor, keeping your head looking forward. Raise your knee off the floor to the point where your right leg is at a forty-five degree angle, then push up with your left foot. Return to the shoulder width stance. Do this exercise very slowly, breaking it down in parts, so that each step is separate. Alternate sides.

Perform all of the following exercises with ankle weights. Do a high number of reps. Work both sides.

Ab/Adductor - Standing sideways and holding something for balance, raise the leg straight up and out towards the ceiling, keeping your knee turned down, (Do not swing! Control the movement). When lowering your leg, cross slightly over your standing leg.

Backward Lifts - Face something solid to hold on to. Stand with your feet shoulder width apart. Lift one leg backward, straight up behind you and toward the ceiling. Raise your foot as high as you can. Bring it down very slowly.

Backward Bends - Face something solid to hold on to. Stand with your feet shoulder width apart bending your leg behind you. Bring your heel up to your buttocks.

Forward Extension - Sit holding the sides of the bench or chair and place a rolled up towel under your knees. Raise one of your legs straight up, out toward the ceiling, letting the balls of your feet graze the floor.

STRENGTH TRAINING: Neck

Do 10-50 of each movement, depending upon your level.

Neck Stretch with Weight - Place a wrap-around neck weight on your head and perform the following:

1. Make circles alternating sides.

2. Push your chin in and out.

3. Make your ear touch your shoulder from side to side.

4. Lower your chin to your chest, then tilt your head to touch the nape of your neck.

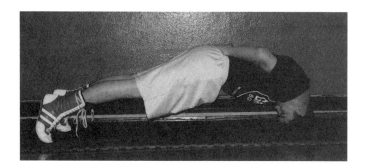

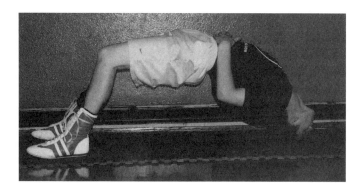

Neck bridge - Place a towel on the floor. Get into the position of a headstand but keep your feet on the floor, up on your toes, making sure your legs are fully extended and your buttocks pointing up in the air. Your hands are resting on your back. Push forward and back with your toes. You can reverse the bridge by placing your hands palm side down at the sides of your head with your elbows pointing up, keeping your feet flat to the floor. Your stomach will be facing upward. Proceed to push forward and backward with your toes. Note: in the reverse bridge, all you are doing is flipping over. **Be extremely careful!**

STRENGTH TRAINING: Wrists

Perform one of the following three exercises.

Keep this note in mind: Take the weight off your lower back and sink into your feet while breathing through the set. Try to let your primary muscles take over.

Silks - Get into a horse stance. Your feet are shoulder width apart, flat to the floor and your buttocks are low. Slightly bend in the waist with your shoulders relaxed. Your arms are slightly bent out in front of you below your chest. To perform, simply open and close your hands rapidly, with a tight grab upon closing, for as many reps as possible. For the last few reps, hold your hands closed for a few seconds before opening them.

Wrist weight hold - Perform this exercise using light weights (1-5 lbs. maximum). Time yourself with a stopwatch increasing the duration each time. Using the same horse stance as for silks. Keep your elbows in and hold a weight in each hand out in front of you, using only your finger tips. Try to just pinch the weight. Hold them until they drop to the floor involuntary.

Stick rotation - Stand with your feet shoulder width apart and your elbows in tight to your body. Hold a stick in one hand in front of you with your palm facing down. Rotate your wrist (turn it) very slowly so your palm faces up, the whole time keeping your wrist straight and the stick level, trying not to let the end of it drop.

Strength Training Combined with Cardiovascular Training

Lesson F. Perform when and if you feel the need for additional strength. I recommend any four exercises for one set. Before beginning, please refer to lesson A.

Upper Body

Complete the following exercises with a partner and a plyometric ball for 3 three-minute rounds. You can perform on the move or standing still. Try mirroring your partner or circling one another. This also can be performed moving forward and backward or side to side.

Note: You can reference *RINGSIDE PRODUCTS* or *USA BOXING* for a complete list of drills.

Forward Push - Stand a comfortable distance apart from each other and push the ball at each other. Elbows are in close to the body and your arms are up. It is most important in this drill to push the ball, not throw it.

Jab - Stand a comfortable distance apart from each other in your boxer's stance. Push the ball at one another as if it were a jab with your elbows held in tight to your body and your hands up high. Throw with the left hand only, use your right hand for balance, and try to recover immediately. Catch the ball as if you were catching a punch in your boxer's stance.

Straight Right - Same as above, except throw the ball at one another as if it were a straight right punch. Throw the ball with the right hand and balance with the left.

Floor Throw - Bounce the ball off the floor to your partner by pushing it out hard and down, making it bounce in the middle between you. Note: do not throw it down making gravity work to your advantage!

The following exercises do not require a plyometric ball. Repeat until failure.

Plyometric Push-Up - Perform the same as a regular push up, except push your entire body off the floor.

Complete the following exercises with dumbbells (1-5 lbs.) at a fast but comfortable pace for one set:

Ski Swings - Standing with your feet shoulder width apart and bending slightly forward, hold weights at your sides vertically with both hands. Raise one arm above your head while the other arm raises backward behind your head simultaneously. Maintain a constant swing.

Sledgehammer - Stand with your feet shoulder width apart in a semi-squat position. Raise the dumbbell with both hands up then lower back down, breaking the momentum of the weight going in one direction by rapidly pulling in the other direction at the last moment. Do not use the lower body. Maintain a constant swing.

69

Side to Side Trunk Swing - Begin in the same stance as above. Holding the weight with both hands vertically at chest level straight out in front of you, proceed to swing the weight from side to side by pulling it.

Do not use your lower body. Maintain a constant motion.

The Fundamentals

Chapter Two

In this Chapter:

Stance and Movement

Defensive Positions

Wrapping the Hands

Pivot & Slide

Equipment list:

Hand-wraps
Maize ball/bag
Mirror
Partner

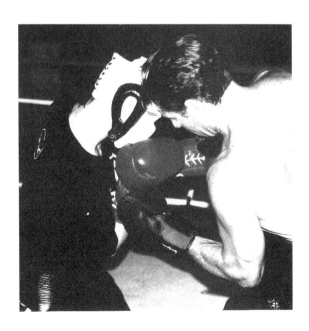

Lesson 1: Stance and Movement

To be accompanied by conditioning A, B, C and D

Right Handed Fighter
"orthodox stance," also called a boxer's stance

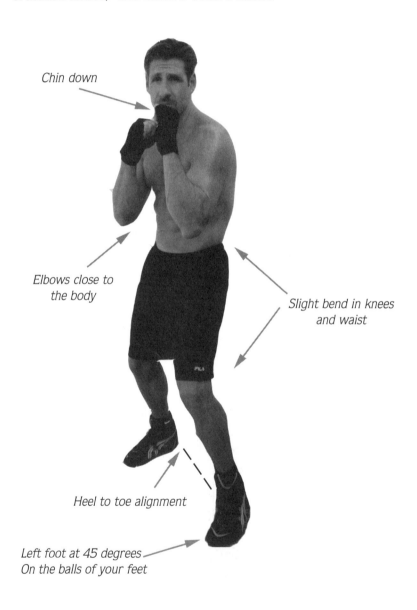

Chin down

Elbows close to the body

Slight bend in knees and waist

Heel to toe alignment

Left foot at 45 degrees
On the balls of your feet

1. Place your left foot forward at a forty-five degree angle, pointing towards your opponent.

2. Your right foot lines up heel to toe at a forty-five degree angle. Both feet shoulder are width apart.

3. Stand up on the balls of your feet. By doing this if you're hit you can fall back on your heels, not the canvas.

4. Slightly bend in your knees and waist. Do not lock your knees.

5. Your shoulder is pointing out in front of you almost as if you're standing sideways. This enables the oncoming punches to go to the sides of you. If you are standing square to your opponent, you become a target. Your shoulder, foot and hip all line up. In essence, you're hiding behind your shoulder.

6. Keep your elbows in tight to your body. This will put you in a natural defensive position to block punches. Always remember there has to be a body behind an elbow. Doing this will also ensure that your body is behind your punch, giving you added power.

7. In making a fist, your thumbs are out resting on top of your fingers between your knuckles and fingernails, with your hands facing one another palm to palm, opened slightly and relaxed, not clinched, at chin level. This will allow you to catch and parry punches away from you.

8. Your arms are bent so your elbows are perpendicular to the floor.

9. Keep your chin down; look out through the top of your eyes like a bull. This will prevent the old one-two (first punch pushes the head back, the other finishes you off).

Left Handed Fighter
unorthodox stance, "southpaw"

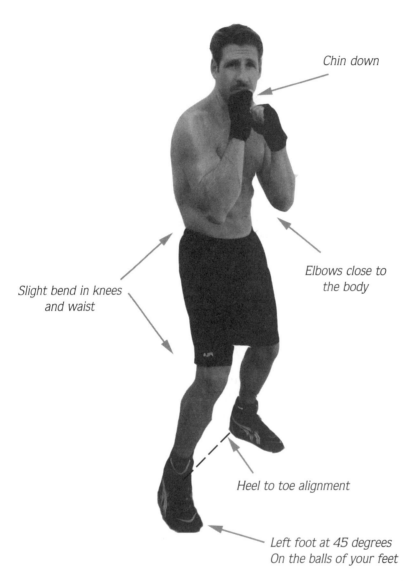

Chin down

Elbows close to
the body

Slight bend in knees
and waist

Heel to toe alignment

Left foot at 45 degrees
On the balls of your feet

Apply everything as in the right handed stance except to the opposite side.

Footwork

Footwork is also known as the "boxer's walk." Boxers should shuffle or glide their feet, the same way a puck travels on an air hockey table. Try not to walk or use a roller-blading motion.

Move your foot closest to the direction you want to move.

Example: If you want to move to the left, move your left foot first. If you want to move to your right, move your right foot first. The same applies for forward and backward movement.

As a boxer, your feet should never cross or come together and touch. When finishing a move always end in your boxer's stance. Remember your left foot doesn't like to be next to your right and your right doesn't like your left foot, so keep them apart.

Back-pedaling: Get up on your toes and move in circles away from your opponent. Try to dig in and push off with your back foot, making 180-degree movements.

PRACTICE: In open, smooth area in front of a mirror.

Lesson 2: Defensive Positions

To be accompanied by conditioning A, B and D

Perform all defensive moves from your boxer's stance.

<u>Duck</u> - Flex & dip your knees slightly. Imagine as if the floor dropped out from under you. Do not lean forward, backward or to either side. Do not drop your head and look down. Keep your eyes on your opponent. This is an advanced technique, because it leaves both hands free to counter.

<u>Catch</u> – With your palms open, simply turn your hand, keeping your hand, arm and elbow tight to body. Never reach for the punch. This defensive technique wears you down because you are absorbing the punches and is limited because it leaves only one hand free to punch. It is a great technique for beginners because it is easy to perform.

<u>Parrying</u> - Simply slap the incoming punch to the side, just before it lands, redirecting it, not absorbing it. Let the momentum bring your opponent off balance. Make sure your arm is very strong, solid and firm when doing this technique. Try not to parry straight rights often. Most of the time they're too powerful. This technique is limited because it leaves only one hand to punch, but it is still very effective.

<u>Step Back Pull</u> - Pull your head and body back away from the punch, moving just one head's width at a time. Little effort is required; it's a safe technique that is advanced, leaving both hands free to counter. (This is my favorite one).

<u>Wall</u> – Touch your right ear with your right glove, by raising your right elbow slightly. This is a great technique for a beginning boxer.

Inside Slip

Outside Slip

<u>Inside / Outside Slip</u> - Slightly bend at the waist and knees. **Inside:** move your head slightly to the left; the incoming punch should go over your right shoulder. **Outside:** move your head slightly to the right; the punch should go over your left shoulder. The distance of a movement to either side should only be a head's width at a time. **Note:** The inside slip, also known, as the "live side" is dangerous because it puts you in harm's way; however, it also leaves you in a great position for counter punching. Slipping to the outside, also known as the "dead side," is a safer move. However you are not left in a position to counter. If you decide to slip to the inside, remember to keep your hands up at all times.

<u>Elbow Blocks</u> - Bend at your knees and waist, moving your body as one unit. Do not drop your arms to the lower portion of your body. Make sure your elbow is pointed at your knees.

<u>Shelling Up</u> - Keep your hands in front of your face with arms and elbows in tight and close to your body. With your chin down, bend over slightly so your elbows are protecting the stomach area while your hands are still held high enough to protect your face and head. Move in, not giving the opponent room to punch. Work at his chest level, aiming towards it. This technique is basic because it is natural instinct to do this. In doing this you will be hit with numerous blows; this technique is usually not recommended for amateurs.

Side U-slip

Forward U-sip

U-Slip - Flex in your knees and waist slightly. Proceed to duck, going down in the shape of the letter U with your body, moving out of the way from the incoming punch. The U-slip can be performed forward or to the side.

<u>Dip</u> – The dip is the same as a slip except you're moving in punching range to the left or right and at the same time moving forward, flexing in the front knee and in your waist. You are on the balls of your feet. At the finish, the punch should go over of your shoulder. In order to perform this you need to time the incoming punch. It can be performed to the left or right side.

Catch (palm-down) – The palm of the glove faces downward with the same side of your body as the incoming punch is thrown. Example: When a punch thrown is a right uppercut, catch with your right palm. Remember: Keep your elbows in tight to your body and do not reach for the incoming punch.

PRACTICE: In front of a mirror, with a partner/coach or maize bag.

Lesson 3: Wrapping the Hands / Pivot & Slide

To be accompanied with conditioning A, B and C

You will need a set of hand wraps (H/w) prior to starting the lesson.

It is very important to wrap your hands prior to putting on any type of glove during training or sparring. (Never hit anything without your hands properly wrapped!)

There are many minute bones in the hands and you need to take every precaution in protecting all of them.

Keep your fingers spread throughout the entire time you're wrapping your hands. Be sure to wrap taut; not too tight or loose.

There are many different methods to wrap your hands. The one below is a simple way that has worked well for me. It is not recommended for a professional bout, but is great for training purposes.

1. Place your thumb through the loop.

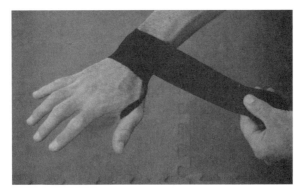

2. Make three circles around your wrist, finishing on the bottom of it. Optional: to include your thumb make two turns around it and proceed to next step.

3. Make three criss-crosses over your hand, one on top of another.

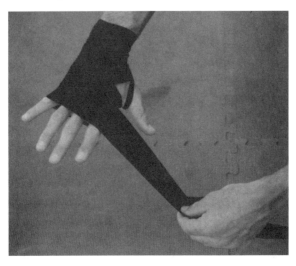

4. Secure it by making one complete circle around your knuckles.

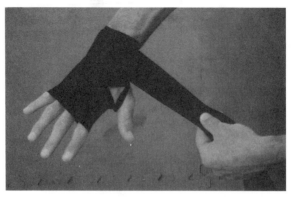

5. Come back over the hand to the wrist and make three more circles around it.

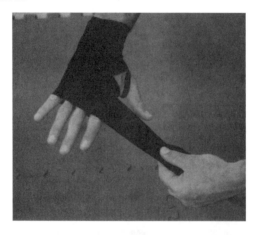

6. Repeat steps three and four.

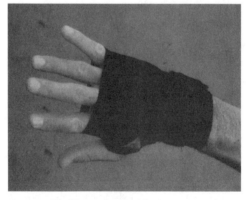

7. Finish the wrap with three more circles around your wrist.

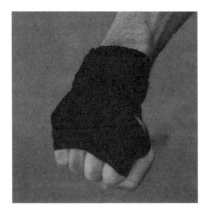

Note: if you have leftover wrap, depending on the length of it, just continue repeating the wrap, except make only one turn around the wrist and one criss-cross, ending wherever it stops.

Pivot & Slide - Also referred to as Circling. This is a defensive technique to keep you in punching range with your opponent. It also can be used offensively to punch at angles and can be used to the left or right.

In your boxer's stance, (1) pivot - turn off the ball of your lead foot and (2) slide.

Pivot & slide simultaneously as fast as you can. Sweep your rear foot around keeping it close to the floor, like the puck on an air hockey table. The lead foot never leaves its original position. You will make a 180-degree turn without disturbing your boxer's stance. You will be facing the other side, balanced and ready to throw punches.

In amateur boxing, you cannot grab your opponent's elbow, head or shoulder, but touching one of those areas would make it easier to perform this technique. However, let the opposing boxer's forward momentum send him / her forward and off balance. Remember, you are blending away from, not opposing, the forward thrust of an oncoming attack.

Pivot & Slide Strategy

1. Use the pivot & slide to keep circling in the center of the ring, warding off punches just like a defensive maneuver.

2. If you are trapped in the corner, use it to get yourself out. Try to time and wait for your opponent's forward momentum along with an incoming right hand.

3. Use it to get off the ropes.

4. Use it in advanced fighting techniques to create and hit at angles.

Rollout: Step to the side, left or right on your toes. This is a combination of side stepping, as in a regular boxer's stance, and backpedaling. It is very similar to pivot & slide, except you're moving out of punching range rapidly. Use this technique when you want distance from your opponent.

PRACTICE: Movement only, on a heavy bag or maize ball, with a partner or coach.

Basic Punches & Strategies

Chapter Three

In this Chapter:

Jab

Bag work: Jabs

Straight Right

Bag work: Straight Right

Rhythm and Style

Hooks

Bag work: Hooks

Equipment list:

16oz. Bag gloves
Double-end bag
Focus pads
Full protective gear
Heavy bag
Speed bag

Lesson 4: Jab

To be accompanied by conditioning A, B, C and D

Punch name: Jab
Punch #: 1, 1b
Equipment needed: Mouthpiece (M/p) H/w 16 oz. Boxing gloves.

OBJECTIVE: Accelerate, turn, recover! The jab is the most frequently thrown punch, used 95% of the time.

Left Jab: Start from your boxer's stance.

1. Throw straight from the chin with the elbow pointed down to the floor.

2. 90% of the time the jab is thrown to the head but it can be thrown at multiple angles.

3. Push off the ball of your right foot. **Note:** for additional power, twist and turn your left hip and buttocks, rapidly and slightly, adding them into the movement.

4. Your shoulders rotate and your hand turns over, so at impact your palm is facing downward to the floor. Your chin is tucked; upon landing your arm is extended, but not to the point of hyperextension. Try to snap it.

5. Exhale during the extension of the punch and inhale on the retraction of the punch (bringing it back, recovering). Breathing through your nose and grunting aloud is always a good thing.

   Note: As your hand leaves its guard position, your fist rotates a quarter notch, gradually closing. Your hand should be completely clenched just before impact. Upon impact, immediately relax and pull it back to the guard position, keeping your wrist straight the entire time.

6. When jabbing to the body, flex and dip your knees slightly. Do not lean forward, backward or to either side. Step into the body keeping the right hand glued to your side and head; act as if the floor dropped out from under you.

Remember: Punch through the opponent! Do not pull the punch or drop the right hand (a common beginner's mistake) or let the left hand lay out there. Never draw your elbow back before initiating the jab. This would alert your opponent to the punch you intend to throw.

1

2

As your hand leaves its guard position, your fist rotates a quarter notch,

Your chin is tucked; upon landing your arm is extended, but not to the point of hyperextension.

Jab Strategy

1. The jab keeps an opponent in a defensive mode, breaking his rhythm and timing. Throwing it does not alter your defensive position or stance so throw it often.

2. Measure distance or drive opponent back with the jab, keeping him off balance, blocking his vision and setting him up so you can create openings and move in to control the bout.

3. Vary the speed of your jab and the placement (moving it up and down) so your opponent cannot time it; this will confuse him.

4. Thrown in multiples the jab can be effectively used to block your opponent's vision with the first punch and land the second or third (double / triple jab).

Practice your jab on both the double end bag and the heavy bag.

Jab Drills

Start in your boxer's stance facing your sparring partner in full protective gear consisting of: mouthpiece, foul protector, headgear, wraps and gloves. Throw at half speed and gradually build up to full speed. Alternate offensive and defensive roles.

Punch Thrown	Punch #	Defense
Jab	1	Duck
Jab	1	Left catch
Jab	1	Inside slip or outside slip
Jab	1	Right parry or outside slip
Jab thrown at 95% speed	1	Left catch
Jab thrown at 80% speed	1	Left catch
Jab thrown at 95% speed	1	Left catch
Jab thrown at 80% speed	1	Left catch
Jab thrown at 70% speed	1	Left catch
Jab	1	Pull
Jab to the body	1-b	Elbow block
Jab	1	Elbow block
Jab to the body	1-b	Left catch

PRACTICE your jabs on heavy bag to start. Additional practices can be completed with the focus pads, double end-bag, shadow boxing, and speed bag.

Lesson 5: Bag Work: Jabs

To be accompanied by conditioning A, B and D

Equipment needed: M/p H/w Bag gloves (B/g)

Perform the following lesson on the heavy bag using only your left hand. If you are a southpaw (left-handed / unorthodox) use your right hand.

Punch Thrown	Punch #	Reps
Jab ¾ speed	1	25-50
Double jab ½ speed	1,1	25-50

From this point throw the following combinations at 100% speed:

Triple jab	1,1,1	25
Jab + Jab to the body	1 1-b	 25
Jab to the body + Jab	1-b 1	 25
Jab + Jab to the body + Jab	1 1-b 1	 10
Jab to the body + Jab + Jab to the body	1-b 1 1-b	 10

Note: You can incorporate focus pads in after the bag work is completed. Also review footwork while throwing punches. Move forward, backward and to the sides.

Lesson 6: Straight Right

To be accompanied by conditioning A, B, C and D

Punch name: Straight Right
Punch #: 2, 2-b
Equipment needed: M/p H/w 16oz.

OBJECTIVE: Accelerate, turn, recover!

Straight right hand:

1. Set the punch up: The straight right is normally thrown after a jab or timed to your opponent's movement. It's a powerful punch! Envision punching through your opponent.

2. Throw straight from the chin. Turn your hand over and fully extended your arm but not to the point of hyperextension. Bring your elbow up to shoulder level keeping your chin tucked down.

3. Your left knee is bent for balance; your hips are squared.

4. Point and throw your right shoulder forward and pivot your hips; your whole body should rotate.

5. Push and pivot off your right foot.

6. Bring your right hand back quickly to your head (recover).

   NOTE: Make sure your elbow points down, not out. Throw the punch straight, not arcing downward. Keep your left hand up. Do not pull your arm back or telegraph the punch by winding up or lifting your elbow.

7. When throwing to the body (2-b), flex and dip your knees slightly. Do not lean backward or to either side. Angle yourself slightly forward and stay low; act as if the floor dropped out from under you.

Your left knee is bent for balance; your hips are squared. At this point you are vulnerable to be hit because your squared off.

1

Point and throw your right shoulder forward and pivot your hips; your whole body should rotate.

2

Turn your hand over and fully extended your arm but not to the point of hyperextension. Bring your elbow up to shoulder level keeping your chin tucked down.

Straight Right Strategy

1. The straight right is usually thrown after a double or triple jab or in a combination. The effect of the first punch should block your opponent's vision or push his head/chin back enabling the right hand to land a solid power punch with the head already back; the effect of the final punch will cause the opponent to go down.

2. Use the straight right as a counter punch after you have made a defensive move or simply countering your opponent's offensive move, trying to catch him off guard in a vulnerable position.

Straight Right Drills

Start in your boxer's stance; face your sparring partner in full protective gear throwing at half speed; gradually build up to full speed. Alternate offensive and defensive roles.

Punch Thrown	Punch #	Defense
Straight right	2	Duck
Straight right	2	Right catch
Straight right	2	Inside slip
Straight right	2	Dip left
Straight right	2	Left parry

At first, practice the straight right on heavy bag and focus pads only. Additional practices can be preformed on the double-end bag, speed bag, and shadow boxing.

Lesson 7: Bag Work: Straight Right

To be accompanied by conditioning A, B and D

Equipment needed: M/p H/w B/g

Perform the following lesson on the heavy bag.

Punch Thrown	Punch #	Reps
Straight right ¾ speed	2	25-50
Double up ¾ speed	2, 2	10

From this point throw the following combinations at 100% speed:

Jab	1	
+ Straight right	2	25
Straight right	2	
+ Jab	1	25
Jab	1	
+ Straight right	2	
+ Jab	1	25
Straight right	2	
+ Jab	1	
+ Straight right	2	25
Straight right	2	
+ Right to the body	2-b	10
Right to the body	2-b	
+ Straight right	2	10

Note: After bag work is complete you can incorporate focus pads into the workout; also review footwork.

Lesson 8: Rhythm and Style

To be accompanied by conditioning A, B, C and D

Equipment needed: M/p H/w

A boxer is never still. He is always in motion making him elusive to hit. When in constant motion, your reflexes have a shorter reaction time. An example is a tennis player: When the server starts to serve, the receiver is already in motion. Much the same, boxing it is like a dance. You must be light, quick and smooth on your feet.

There are two types of rhythm: Side to Side and Back and Forth. The student can learn both or which ever feels more natural to him or her.

Side to Side is an inside/outside or U slip with an added movement of a bounce in the lower body.

Back and Forth is a pull with an added bounce in the waist, legs, feet and knees.

There are also two types of boxing styles: There is the "Boxer" and there is the "Bull" (brawler). Do not try to be either; your natural talent and form will develop on its own. A good fighter can adopt, adjust and overcome any style he is up against by becoming some-thing like a chameleon.

Boxer – Someone who is quick on their feet, up on their toes, usually with a back and forth rhythm, who likes to stick and move and also uses range fighting. Examples: Muhammad Ali, Roy Jones Jr. Sugar Ray Leonard, Pernell Whitaker and Lennox Lewis.

Bull / Slugger – Someone who is flat-footed, likes to cut the ring off, favors inside fighting and countering, almost always a powerful puncher. Examples: Joe Frazier, David Tua.

Introduction to Speed Bag Work

Strike the bag at chin height, punching through the bag and keeping your hands up the entire time using:

1. Left hits only.

2. Right hits only.

3. Left and right hits.

4. Over-under: strike the bag with your fist below the pinky finger, turn and roll your hand over and strike the bag backhand (over & under).

Note: After you have completed the lesson, you can choose between the following: bag work, focus pads or review any previous lesson that you feel you need to improve on.

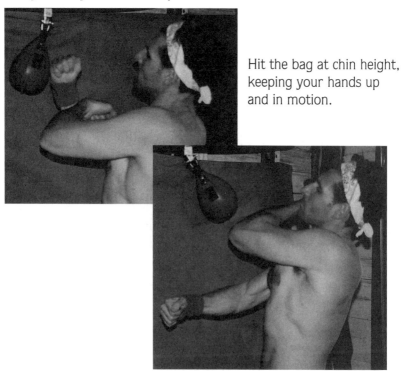

Hit the bag at chin height, keeping your hands up and in motion.

Lesson 9: Hooks

To be accompanied by conditioning A, B and D

Punch name: Hooks
Punch #: 3, 3-b & 4, 4-b
Equipment needed: M/p H/w 16oz.

Left Hook: Start from your boxer's stance.

1. 80 percent of the time this punch will be thrown from an inside position. Dip your elbow towards your hip.

2. Transfer your weight to the left foot.

3. Pivot on the ball of your left foot from 6 o'clock to 3 o'clock, as if you were stepping on ants.

4. Turn and rotate your hips and torso quickly.

5. Your arm does not move independently from your body. Your forearm is parallel to the ground and your elbow moves as one with your hips.

6. Keep your palm facing down for close range and facing in for a distant hook. This can go either way; whichever feels natural to you.

7. Keep it a short compact six-inch punch with your arm bent, forming the shape of a hook.

8. Tuck the punch into your chest upon completion.

   Note: When throwing to the body, flex and dip your knees slightly. Make sure you do not draw back, loop, or extend your arm far from your body like a roundhouse punch. Also do not throw the hook too close to your opponent or you will wind up hugging him. (**Right Hook:** Same method applies)

Your forearm is parallel to the ground and your elbow moves as one with your hips.

Pivot on the ball of your left foot from 6 o'clock to 3 o'clock.

Keep it a short compact six-inch punch with your arm bent, forming the shape of a hook. Tuck the punch into your chest upon completion.

Hook Strategy

1. Never lead with a left or right hook. It leaves you in a compromising position.

2. Try to work your left hook off a jab, straight right or uppercut. This will put your opponent's chin/head in the proper target zone for a knockdown.

3. Try not to throw right hooks if you're right-handed. Your natural position causes your hand to be too far away from your opponent thus leaving you vulnerable after you throw it.

4. Try to catch your opponent moving backward or forward. This will add to the power of the punch.

5. The hook travels outside your opponent's range of vision. By doing this it will catch him by surprise.

6. Double up on hooks. This will cause your opponent not to see or expect the second; again use the element of surprise.

7. Try to move the hooks up and down on the body; it is harder to defend that way and will create an opening.

8. Use it after you slip a punch, which puts you in a great position to throw a hook.

Practice moving your hooks up and down the body.

Hook Drills

Start in your boxer's stance and face each other in full protective gear, throwing at half speed, gradually building up to full speed. Alternate offensive and defensive roles.

Punch Thrown	Punch #	Defense
Left hook	3	Right wall
Left hook	3	Duck
Left hook	3	U slip left
Left hook	3	Dip right
Left hook	3-b	Right elbow block

PRACTICE on heavy bag, focus pads, speed and double-end bag, and shadow boxing.

Practice your hooks on the focus pads and the heavy bag.

Lesson 10: Bag Work: Hooks

To be accompanied by conditioning A, B, and D

Equipment needed: M/p H/w & B/g

Perform the following lesson on the heavy bag at full speed.

Punch Thrown	Punch #	Reps
Left hook to the head	3	25-50
Left hook to the body	3-b	25-50
Right hook to the head	4	25-50
Right hook to the body	4-b	25-50
Left hook to the body + Left hook	3-b 3	25
Left hook + Left hook to the body	3 3-b	25
Right hook to the head	4	10
Right hook to the body	4-b	10
Right hook + Right hook to the body	4 4-b	10
Right hook to the body + Right hook	4-b 4	10
Left hook + Right hook	3 4	10

Punch Thrown	Punch #	Reps
Right hook	4	
+ Left hook	3	10
Left hook	3	
+ Right hook	4	
+ Left hook to the body	3-b	
+ Right hook to the body	4-b	10
Left hook to the body	3-b	
+ Right hook to the body	4-b	
+ Left hook	3	
+ Right hook	4	10
Left hook to the body	3-b	
+ Right hook	4	10

Note: Upon completion, proceed to the double end bag and repeat the workout with a slight variation: incorporate inside and outside (distant) hooks. Also incorporate punch # 1 and # 2 into the workout. Focus pads may be added in to the workout.

Advanced Punches & Strategies

Chapter Four

In this Chapter:

Neutralizing your Opponent

Uppercut

Bag work: Uppercuts

Defensive Positioning

Additional Punches

Bag work: Additional Punches

Shadowboxing

Equipment list:

uppercut bag

Lesson 11: Neutralizing your Opponent

To be accompanied by conditioning A, B, C, and D

The goal here is to neutralize your opponent's strengths while taking full advantage of his/her weaknesses; exploit it!

1. <u>TALL OPPONENT:</u> Line your left foot outside his left foot and use angles moving to the left/right. Make him come to you. If he refuses to, make sure you go in behind your jab, moving it up and down, throwing lots of hooks and uppercuts to the body, trying to get under him, especially on the ropes. Most importantly: never go straight back. Move left or right and don't get stuck caught on the ropes.

2. <u>BULL/RUSHER:</u> Pivot and slide constantly, giving him lots of angles. If he gets in on you, "shell-up" and step in, giving him no room to punch.

3. <u>JABBER:</u> Keep your guard up with your right hand held high. Try to keep moving and do not allow yourself to be a stationary target. Jabbers are usually fast handed and quick, so move in and work the body, cutting off the ring.

4. <u>HEAVY HITTER / SLUGGER</u>: Keep moving with angles, not letting him/her get set to punch. Stick and move. As soon as you hit the ropes, pivot & slide instantly.

5. <u>SOUTHPAW:</u> Make them come to you and always circle to your left. They have very powerful left hands, so catch strong with your right hand. Their defense is open to a right cross.

6. <u>SHORT OPPONENT:</u> Box tall making them punch up. When you're in close, pull their head down (do not let the referee see this). Most of the time they have short arms, so use range fighting, making sure to get a full extension on your jab.

7. <u>BOXER:</u> Cut the ring off, trying to force them to the ropes, watching and attacking their body in close. Do not punch when you're moving in. This is what they want you to do so they can pull and stick you. If all fails and you have the ability to box back, do so. Boxers hate this; it frustrates them to be beat at their own game.

8. <u>CLINCHER:</u> Every time they move in, step back or to the side and punch! If they tie you up, throw many punches down the middle until the referee steps in and breaks it up (punch-out).

POINTS TO REMEMBER IN THE RING:

1. Relax, use your head and stay calm; breathe deeply.

2. Show confidence at all times.

3. Punch when in range only.

4. Keep your body and head moving (rhythm).

5. Hands held high; chin down.

6. Show different looks; try to confuse your opponent.

7. When your opponent is set to hit, move!

8. Remember: he or she is just as tired as you are.

Notes on Inside Fighting:

I do not recommend inside fighting in amateur boxing because body punches show their effects late in a fight (usually rounds 7, 8, and 9). Also it's harder for judges to see the punches landing cleanly and in some events they do not count as points. However, inside fighting is a very important part of being a boxer and worth going over the strategy (science of it). If you wish to pursue this style of fighting, it is recommended to:

1. Stay lower than your opponent when in close range.

2. Target the body to set up the head.

3. Stay in your optimal hitting distance at all times (not too close and not too far).

4. Throw short punches.

5. Be very busy (throw many punches at a quick pace).

6. Keep your hands held high.

7. Use lots of head movement.

8. Stay with your opponent, using quick turns (pivot & slide in range).

9. If your opponent stays in the center of ring, do not provide a stationary target. Remember that there are no ropes for him to lean back on, so press forward.

PRACTICE: After reviewing the above strategies, hit the speed bag for four rounds.

Lesson 12: Uppercuts

To be accompanied by conditioning A, B and D

Punch name: Uppercuts
Punch #: 5, 6
Equipment needed: M/p H/w 16oz.

Left Uppercut:

Start from your boxer's stance.

1. Uppercuts are usually thrown following jabs or hooks from close range.

2. Dip almost to your hip, lower your left shoulder and transfer your weight to the left side.

3. Push off the ball of your left foot while rotating your hips.

4. Keep your arms bent in the shape of the letter (V) with your palm facing you.

5. Bring the power from your legs and hips into the upward thrust.

   Note: Do not draw back your elbow or wind up your arm; also make sure your arm does not drop below your waist.

Right Uppercut:

Same as above applies except dip and transfer your weight to the right side. Lower your right-shoulder and push off the ball of your right foot.

Keep your arm bent in the shape of a V.

Bring the power from your legs and hips into the upward thrust.

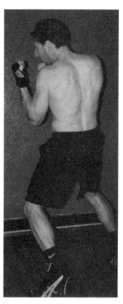

1

2

For the right uppercut, lower your right-shoulder and push off the ball of your right foot.

Bring the power from your legs and hips into the upward thrust

1

2

Uppercut Strategy

1. Uppercuts to the chin stand up an opponent giving you a target: the head. This puts your opponent in a position where successive punches will knock him or her down.

2. Follow a right uppercut to the chin with a left hook to the head because the uppercut lifts the chin and head back giving you a target and again putting him in a natural position to go down.

3. Uppercuts to the body cause an opponent to lean forward. Step back and follow with an uppercut to the head. This will cause his weight transfer to go in different directions, throwing off his equilibrium.

Practice your uppercuts on the focus pads and heavy bag.

Uppercut Drills

Start in your boxer's stance; face each other in full protective gear, throwing at half speed. Gradually build up to full speed, Alternate offensive and defensive roles.

Punch Thrown	Punch #	Defense
Left uppercut	5	Right elbow block
Right uppercut	6	Left elbow block
Left uppercut	5	Right palm catch
Right uppercut	6	Left palm catch
Left uppercut	5	Step back or pull
Right uppercut	6	Step back or pull

PRACTICE on an uppercut bag, double-end bag or heavy bag. Also include focus pads and shadow boxing.

The uppercut bag is specially designed for practicing this punch.

Lesson 13: Bag Work: Uppercuts

To be accompanied by conditioning A, B, C and D

Equipment needed: M/p H/w B/g

Perform this lesson at 100% speed.

Punch Thrown	Punch #	Reps
Left uppercut	5	25-50
Right uppercut	6	25-50
Left uppercut +Right uppercut	5 6	25
Right uppercut +Left uppercut	6 5	25
Jab +Left uppercut	1 5	10
Jab +Left uppercut +Right uppercut	1 5 6	10
Jab +Right uppercut	1 6	10
Left hook to the body +Right hook to the body +Left uppercut +Right uppercut	3-b 4-b 5 6	10
Left uppercut +Left uppercut	5 5	10

Punch Thrown	Punch #	Reps
Right uppercut	6	
+Right uppercut	6	10
Left uppercut	5	
+Right uppercut	6	
+Left uppercut	5	10
Right uppercut	6	
+Right uppercut	6	
+Right uppercut	6	
+Left hook	3	5
Right uppercut	6	
+Left hook	3	
+Right hook	4	5
Left uppercut	5	
+Right hook	4	
+Left hook	3	5

Upon conclusion, review footwork, rhythm and style.

Lesson 14: Defensive Positioning

To be accompanied by conditioning A, B and D

Equipment needed: M/p H/w B/g

Start in your boxer's stance; face each other in full protective gear, throwing at half speed. Gradually build up to full speed,

Punch Thrown	Punch #	Defense
Jab	1	Duck
Jab	1	Right parry - Outside slip
Jab	1	Right catch
Jab	1	Inside slip or outside slip
Straight right	2	Duck
Straight right	2	Right catch
Straight right	2	Inside slip
Straight right	2	Dip left
Straight right	2	Left parry – outside slip
Left hook	3	Right wall
Left hook	3	Duck
Left hook	3	U slip left
Left hook to the body	3-b	Right elbow block
Right hook to the body	4-b	Left elbow block

PRACTICE: pivot & slide with a partner, heavy bag and maize ball.

Lesson 15: Additional Punches

To be accompanied by conditioning A, B, C and D

Punch name: Up Jab
Punch #: 1-up
Equipment needed: M/p H/w 16oz.

OBJECTIVE: Accelerate, recover!

Starting from your boxer's stance, or as you backpedal, circle/side-step or even retreat.

1. Similar to the hook, this is a punch thrown with the element of surprise. With your left hand at your waist, raise it to your opponent as if you were shaking hands.

2. Your left shoulder is pointing to your opponent, so you are able to lead and hide behind it.

3. The punch is thrown at full speed, then snapped back. It's aimed directly at the front target. Or it can be thrown almost backhand ("flick it"), aimed at a side target

Up Jab Strategy

1. The up jab is effective at finding the hole or gap in the defense because it can be thrown from multiple angles. This will enable you to open up and create openings in a tight well-defended opponent.

2. Used offensively, it controls the tempo. Used also to explore (probe).

3. Defensively, it's used while circling or backpedaling to keep the opponent away from you.

4. The up jab breaks the opponent's rhythm, causing his timing to go off. This strategy can be used offensively or defensively.

PRACTICE: On a heavy bag, double-end bag and focus pads, or in shadow boxing.

1   2   3

With your left hand at your waist, raise it to your opponent as if you were shaking hands.

Use your shoulder to hide behind.

Overhand Right

Punch name: Overhand right
Punch #: 2-high
OBJECTIVE: Accelerate, turn, recover!

Start from your boxer's stance.

1. The overhand right is a straight punch that has to go over the top of incoming jab in an arc. It is not a roundhouse punch.

2. When you throw the punch, your right shoulder will rise naturally; hide behind it.

3. Move your head to the left.

4. Dip your left knee and shoulder.

5. For the finish, rotate and extend your arm while turning your hand over.

1 **2**

When you throw the punch, your right shoulder will rise naturally; hide behind it. Move your head to the left. Dip your left knee and shoulder.

For the finish, rotate and extend your arm while turning your hand over.

Overhand Right Strategy

1. Try to use the overhand right with the element of surprise.

2. Time the incoming jab, so that you can throw the overhand right over the top.

3. The overhand right is a great punch to throw in a combination, for example, 1, 2-high, 5.

PRACTICE: On a heavy bag, double-end bag, focus pads or shadow boxing,

Practice the overhand right on the focus pads.

121

Right Cross

Punch name: Right Cross
Punch #: 2-cross
OBJECTIVE: Accelerate, turn, recover!

Start from your boxer's stance.

1. The right cross is the same punch as a straight right, except it continues through even further across your body.

2. Turn more of your right shoulder, almost to the point where the left shoulder is behind you and you are leading (pointing) with the right shoulder.

3. The target also changes; it becomes the side of the head or chest, as opposed to the straight right, where it is the front of the head (face) or the chest.

1

2

Turn more of your right shoulder, almost to the point where the left shoulder is behind you and you are leading with the right shoulder.

Right Cross Strategy

1. The cross is a good punch to use to mix up your opponent. He may confuse it with a straight right.

2. It works well against a southpaw (unorthodox) fighter because they are slightly off center to your left, causing their chin to be directly in the path of the punch.

3. Like the straight right, it's a very powerful punch.

PRACTICE: On a heavy bag, double-end bag and focus pads or shadow box.

Lesson 16: Bag Work

To be accompanied by conditioning A, B and D

Equipment needed: M/p H/w B/g

Perform on a heavy bag at full speed.

Punch Thrown	Punch #	Reps
Up-Jab	1-Up	25
Overhand right	2-h	25
Right cross	2-c	25
Jab +Overhand right	1 2-h	25
Jab +Right cross	1 2-c	25.
Jab +Right cross +Left hook	1 2-c 3	10
Jab +Overhand right +Left uppercut	1 2-h 5	5
Up-Jab +Jab	1-Up 1	5
Jab +Up-Jab	1 1-Up	5

Punch Thrown	Punch #	Reps
Jab	1	
+Up-Jab	1-Up	
+Jab	1	5
Up-Jab	1-Up	
+Jab	1	
+Up-Jab	1-Up	5

Upon conclusion, review footwork, rhythm and styles.

Practice your combinations on the focus pads and heavy bag.

Lesson 17: Shadowboxing

To be accompanied by conditioning A, B and C

Equipment needed: M/p H/w

Duration: Up to fifteen minutes without stopping (nonstop punching). Advanced workout: up to thirty minutes.

Perform the lesson with a hand weight (ranging from ½ to 5 lbs) held in each hand (optional). Remember to add defensive movement into the routine. Staying in a rhythm, you can also add to any combination.

Start in your boxer's stance. Have the instructor call out the following punches:

Punches Thrown	Punch #'s
Jab	1
Double Jab	1,1
Triple Jab	1,1,1
Jab • Jab to the body	1, 1-b
Jab • Jab to the body • Jab	1,1-b,1
Jab • Jab • Jab to the body	1,1,1-b
Jab to the body • Jab	1-b,1
Jab to the body • Jab • Jab to the body	1-b,1,1-b
Jab • Straight right	1,2
Jab • Straight right • Jab	1,2,1
Jab • Jab • Straight right	1,1,2
Jab • Straight right • Jab • Straight right	1,2,1,2
Jab • Right cross • Jab	1,2-c,1
Straight right • Jab	2,1
Straight right • Jab • Straight right	2,1,2
Straight right • Straight right	2,2

Punches Thrown	Punch #'s
Jab • Right to the body	1,2-b
Right to the body • Left hook	2-b,3
Jab • Right to the body • Left hook	1,2-b,3
Jab • Right to the body • Left hook • Right hook	1,2-b,3,4
Jab • Left uppercut • Straight right	1,5,2
Straight right • Left uppercut • Right uppercut	2,5,6
Jab • Overhand right	1,2-h
Jab • Overhand right • Left uppercut	1,2-h,5
Jab to the body • Overhand right	1-b,2-h
Jab • Left hook	1,3
Jab • Left uppercut	1,5
Jab • Left hook • Left uppercut	1,3,5
Jab • Left uppercut • Left hook	1,5,3
Jab • Straight right • Left hook	1,2,3
Jab • Left hook to body • Left hook	1,3-b,3
Jab • Straight right • Left hook • Right hook	1,2,3,4,
Right to the body • Left hook	2-b,3
Right to the body • Left hook to body • Left hook	2-b,3-b,3
Left hook • Left hook	3,3
Right hook • Right hook	4,4
Left hook to body • Right hook • Left hook • Right hook to body	3-b,4,3,4-b
Left hook • Left hook to body • Left hook	3,3-b,3
Right uppercut • Left hook	6,3
Right uppercut • Right uppercut • Right uppercut • Left hook	6,6,6,3
Left uppercut • Straight right	5,2
Left uppercut • Right uppercut	5,6,
Right uppercut • Left uppercut	6,5

Punches Thrown	**Punch #'s**
Left uppercut • Right uppercut • Left uppercut	5,6,5,
Right uppercut • Left uppercut • Right uppercut	6,5,6

Remember: Punches become more powerful as they are added on to the combination. The first one or two punches are usually the set up punches.

Right uppercut • Right uppercut	6,6,
Left uppercut • Left uppercut	5,5,
Jab • Right uppercut • Left hook	1,6,3
Jab • Left hook to body • Left hook • Straight right	1,3-b,3,2
Jab • Left hook • Straight right • Left hook to body	1,3,2,3-b
Straight right • Left hook • Straight right	2,3,2
Left hook • Straight right • Left hook	3,2,3

Jab • Straight right • Left hook • Right hook • Left uppercut • Right uppercut	1,2,3,4,5,6,
Jab • Straight right • Left hook • Right hook • Left uppercut • Right uppercut • Left hook • Right hook	1,2,3,4,5,6,3,4
Jab • Left hook • Right hook	1,3,4
Jab • Left hook to body • Right hook	1,3-b,4
Jab • Right uppercut • Left uppercut • Left uppercut • Left hook	1,6,5,4,3

Try to avoid your punches being timed by varying the speed of them. Also move your punches up and down (head-body, body-head). One punch should set up the next naturally, letting your feet follow the opponent. As the punches connect, stay on top of opponent.

Defensive Tactics

Chapter Five

In this Chapter:

Lesson 18: Countering Off 1 Punch

To be accompanied by conditioning A, B and D

Equipment needed: M/p H/w 16oz.

Start in your boxer's stance, face each other in full protective gear, throwing at half speed. Gradually build up to full speed.

Punch Thrown	#	Defense	Counterpunch	#
Jab	1	Right-catch	Jab	1
Jab	1	Outside slip	Jab	1
Jab	1	Outside slip	Overhand right	2-h
Jab	1	Parry down left	Jab	1
Jab	1	Inside slip	Overhand right	2-h
Jab	1	Left parry	Jab, Straight right	1, 2
Jab	1	Right parry	Jab, Straight right	1, 2
Jab	1	Inside slip	Left hook, Right (body)	3, 2-b
Jab	1	Outside slip	Jab, Right uppercut	1, 6
Jab	1	Pull	L. hook, Straight right	3, 2
Jab	1	Dip left	Right to body	2-b
			+Left hook to body	3-b
			+Right to body,	2-b
			+Left hook to body	3-b
			+Left hook	3

Punch Thrown	#	Defense	Counterpunch	#
Double jab	1, 1	R. catch, Pull	Straight right	2
Jab to body	1-b	Pull	Jab, Straight right	1, 2
Jab to body	1-b	Right parry or elbow block	Straight right	2

PRACTICE any or all lessons that you feel may need to develop further.

Lesson 19: Ring Tactics

To be accompanied by conditioning A, B, C and D

Equipment needed: M/p H/w 16oz.

Clinch

Place your arms around your opponent's shoulders with your biceps touching him as you pull them into you (not using your hands). Have your arms slide down to his elbows, keeping your head up over his shoulder, not on it. If you're on the ropes or in the corner, spin him fast and hard. Keep your hands up on the break.

STRATEGY: This technique is done when you're fighting close (inside fighting: review Lesson # 11) and want to stop your opponent from punching. It is also used when you're trapped on the ropes and cannot successfully use another technique; simply clinch (tie them up), the referee will step in and break the hold allowing you to get out/off the ropes. Another opportunity to use this technique is when you are fighting a very hard puncher with lots of power; stay very close to him not allowing him any arm motion/extension so he can not gain any forward momentum on his punches. Every-time he throws, step in and clinch (hold him).

DRILL: Practice with a partner, in the center of the ring, on the ropes and in the corner. Take turns being the clincher. Mix and match partners if possible so that you can work with different body types.

Cutting off the Ring

Imagine the ring divided into boxes, like a cross where the lines meet in the center of the ring (+). Never let your opponent turn and cross a line. Cut him off by mirroring, not following him. Stay even with him and stop his movement by throwing hooks in the direction he wants to move (hook him off). When you have him in the corner think of a triangle and keep him contained in it. Also give him small boxes to work in, not allowing room for him to roll out. If he turns a corner and passes over your imaginary line, immediately adjust and start a new one. Move forward and to the side, not backward.

STRATEGY: This technique is used to slow down and contain a fighter (trapping him) with a boxer's style, so you're able to catch him. It is very effective at taking the ring away from him, so he is unable to stick-and-move or range fight you. Control the real estate in the ring!

DRILL: Practice in groups of two; keep rotating so everyone has a chance to work with different body styles. Let one student be the boxer, the other the bull/slugger, cutting off the ring. Play a game: Every time the boxer turns a corner, he gets a point. The first one to reach three, wins. Keep taking turns, giving each partner one minute to earn a point. Keep the punching very light; this is not a hitting drill!

Pair up and practice cutting off the ring.

Feinting

Fake a hit to one area of the body (head/abdomen) then hit in a different area. It's all about deceiving your opponent. You hope he goes to adjust his defense, or does the offensive move you're drawing him to do so you can exploit the new found opening. To do this you will need to use your eyes, hands, body, legs, facial expressions and sound all as decoys, alone and in unison.

PRACTICE in front of a mirror. Examples: fake a 1 and throw a 2. Draw back a 2 causing him/her to move to the right and throw a 3. Fake a 1 very high and throw a 1b.

Lesson 20: Punches/Footwork Review

To be accompanied by conditioning A, B and D

Equipment needed: M/p H/w B/g

Review of Punches

Review the instructions on each punch. Practice each of the following punches and footwork skills in front of a mirror.

Practice on any of the following: heavy or speed bag, double-end bag, focus pads.

1	Jab to the chin
1-b	Jab to the body
2	Straight right to the chin
2-b	Right to the body
3	Hook to the head
3-b	Hook to the body
4	Hook to the head
4-b	Hook to the body
5	Left uppercut
6	Right uppercut
1-up	Jab from the waist
2-c	Right cross
2-h	Overhand right

Review of Footwork

DRILL: Perform 3, three-minute rounds of footwork drills in the ring reviewing the following footwork:

In & out (forward/backward)

Backpedaling

Side to side

Left to right

Circling

Cutting off ring

Free-style

Lesson 21: Review of Defenses

To be accompanied by conditioning A, B, C and D

Equipment needed: M/p H/w 16oz.

Practice each of the following defensive techniques with a slip-bag (maize ball), partner or coach.

Start from a boxer's stance:

Duck

Catch

Parry

Pull

Inside-outside/slip

Shelling- up

Wall

U-slip: Forward & side to side

Elbow-blocks: left & right

Dips: left & right.

Catch: palm-down left & right

Pivot & slide: left & right

Practice your defensive techniques with a slip-bag (maize-ball).

DRILL – Enter the ring for 3, three-minute rounds of just defense combined with footwork.

Complete the lesson with one round of freestyle shadow boxing. (Offense/defense & footwork incorporated).

Practice using only defense and footwork, such as the pull (right) and U-Slip (below).

Lesson 22: Introduction to Sparring

To be accompanied by conditioning A, B and D

Equipment needed: Both boxers are in full protective gear.

Note: Spar only if you feel you are "truly" ready. Remind yourself that it's optional. You do not have to enter the ring, unless you feel you want to at this point.

1. Box for a duration of 3, two-minute rounds, with a one-minute rest period in between. If agreed upon by both boxers, continue a few more rounds.

2. Throw only left hands at half speed, using right hands defensively only.

3. Incorporate all of the acquired skills to this point.

POINTS TO REMEMBER:

1. Breathe and stay relaxed.

2. Keep your chin down and eyes on the opponent at all times. Never turn your back.

3. Keep your composure and stay in control at all times (showing no anger).

4. Always enter the ring with an objective and strategy.

THREE COMMON MISTAKES TO BE AWARE OF:

1. **Holding your hands too low.** Try to frequently touch your headgear around your ear, forehead, temple and upper cheek bone with your gloves. Doing this reaffirms that your hands are up protecting your face and head.

2. **Holding your breath as you punch** will cause you to have less power and tire you out quickly. Try to breathe through your nose.

3. **Not having a body behind your elbows** will cause you to lose power and will give your opponent openings to land punches. Frequently bang your sides (oblique) and upper hip with the inner part of your elbows, biceps and forearms.

PRACTICE: on focus pads.

Begin sparring in a controlled environment under the supervision of your coach or instructor.

Lesson 23: Countering Off One Punch

To be accompanied by conditioning A, B, C and D

Equipment needed: M/p H/w 16oz.

Start in boxer's stance. Face each other in full protective gear, throwing at half speed. Gradually build to full speed.

Punch	#	Defense	Counterpunch	#
Straight right	2	Right catch	Straight right	2
Straight right	2	Left parry	Jab, Straight right	1, 2
Straight right	2	Pull	Jab, Straight right	1, 2
Straight right	2	Left parry	L. uppercut, Str. right	5,2
Straight right	2	Left catch	L. hook, Straight right	3, 2
Straight right	2	Outside slip	L. hook, L. hook-body	3, 3-b
Straight right	2	Dip left	Right to body, L. hook	2-b, 3
Straight right	2	Dip right	Jab-body, Ovrhd right	1-b, 2-h
Straight right	2	Inside slip	Jab-body, Jab, R. hook	1-b, 1, 4
Straight right	2	Outside slip	L. hook, Right to body, Straight right	3, 2-b, 2
Right to body	2-b	Left parry	Straight right, L. hook	2,3
Right to body	2-b	Pull	Jab, Straight right	1, 2
Right to body	2-b	Right elbow	Right uppercut	6

Punch	#	Defense	Counterpunch	#
Right to body	2-b	Left elbow	Right hook	4
Right to body	2-b	Right elbow	Left hook	3
Right to body	2-b	Left elbow	Straight right	2

PRACTICE shadow boxing in front of a mirror.

Lesson 24: Countering Off One Punch

To be accompanied by conditioning A, B, and D

Equipment needed: M/p H/w 16oz.

Start in boxer's stance. Face each other in full protective gear, throwing at half speed. Gradually build to full speed.

Punch	#	Defense	Counterpunch	#
Left hook	3	Right wall	L. hook, R. hook	3,4
Left hook	3	Right wall	Jab	1
Left hook	3	Right wall	Left hook	3
Left hook	3	Right wall	Jab, Left hook	1, 3
L. hook-body	3-b	Pull	Jab, Straight right	1, 2
L. hook-body	3-b	Right elbow	Right hook, Left hook, Right uppercut	4, 3, 6
Left uppercut	5	Pull	Straight Right	2
R. uppercut	6	Right elbow	R. hook-body, R. hook	4-b, 4
R. uppercut	6	Pull	Jab	1

PRACTICE shadow boxing in front of a mirror.

Lesson 25: Handicap Sparring

To be accompanied by conditioning A, B, C and D).

Equipment required: Both boxers are in full protective gear.

1. Spar 4 two minute rounds or more at half speed.

2. Have one boxer on offense and the other boxer on defense. Switch each round.

3. A coach or trainer should call out punches (from the number system) to be thrown.

4. The boxer on defense should practice tying up (clinching), pivoting & sliding and using the entire range of defensive techniques.

End the workout with the coach putting on gloves and telling you exactly what punch he is going to throw at you (prior to throwing it). You will use the appropriate defensive technique.

Advanced sparring games: Performed at the repeat of the program.

1. Role-play: One fighter plays the bull/slugger and the other a boxer. Alternate each round.

2. Have one boxer throw both hands while the other throws only left hands. Have both boxers throw only right hands. Have boxers throw only one type of punch (any).

Boxing: The American Martial Art

For The Instructor

Chapter Six

In this Chapter:

Lesson Notes

Punch Number Handout

First Day Handout

Parents' Handout

Final Note to the Instructor

Boxing is a wonderful tool if presented in a structured, organized program. The student can obtain many positive qualities from it such as a positive release of energy and sometimes frustration. By controlling anger and aggression a boxer can gain a strong sense of self worth which comes from advancing in skill level. The character that is built through confidence and discipline gives the student high self-esteem, which can be used years later down the path of life.

Although one would not think so, boxers also achieve teamwork. They are building a sense of camaraderie among the people in the gym. They become a family. When you go on the road traveling, the people in your gym are all you have. When sparring, it brings closeness between two individuals, through mutual respect. I always say "Sparring Partners" not "Opponents". You are across from each other in the ring to help one another grow in all aspects. Least of all let's not forget this is not just for controlling anger, aggression, or frustrations, this program has the same positive effects on a timid under-aggressive person. It is truly amazing. There are not enough words to describe the athletic, cardiovascular and overall body strength and stamina you acquire.

In conclusion, I truly hope this book helps you achieve your goals. If you have material you feel would enhance the routine by adding it, do so. If you feel the need to omit or modify something, do so. I strongly recommend that both the instructor and student become members of *U.S.A. Boxing.*

We learn from one another. The student teaches the teacher, as well as the teacher teaching the student. The book I have created on these pages is not intended to replace the instructor/coach, but is a supplement to help as a guide. If you have any questions or comments, I can be reached through my email address: miketenacity@juno.com

Notes on the Lessons

A demonstration is required for the following lessons:

1   # 2   # 4   # 6   # 8   # 9   # 11   # 12
15   # 19

A lecture is required for the following lessons:

14   # 11

For **Lesson 22: Introduction to Sparring**, I advise the Instructor/ coach to be in the ring with the boxers. Remember to look in their eyes making sure they're not glassy and they are coherent. Close supervision is required!

Common mistakes a coach should look for with inexperienced students:

1. No body behind the elbows.
2. Dropping the right hand when the left is thrown.
3. Dropping the left hand when the right is thrown.
4. Holding the breath.
5. Not breathing from the nose.
6. Hands held low, dropping them.
7. When a punch is thrown at him/her, the boxer puts out both hands to block or throws themselves with both hands.
8. Squaring off to the opponent.
9. Pulling, drawing or winding up of punches.
10. Flinching.
11. Excessive bouncing or moving around
12. Rule breaking.

Handout: Punch Numbering System

For the student to memorize after Lesson 8 (mandatory).

Jab = # 1
Jab to the body = # 1-b
Double jab = # 1,1
Triple jab = #1,1,1
Up jab = # 1-up

Straight right = # 2
Right to the body = # 2-b
Over the top overhand right = # 2-high
Right cross = # 2-cross

Left hook = # 3
 Left hook to the body = # 3-b

Right hook = # 4
Right hook to the body = # 4-b

Left uppercut = # 5
Left uppercut to the chin = # 5-high

Right uppercut = # 6
Right uppercut to the chin = # 6-high

Handout: First Day Questions

Distribute to the student at the start of the program (optional).

Answer the following questions in your own words.

1. What drew you to the sport of Amateur Boxing?

2. Why do you want to learn how to box?

3. What would be some of the things you hope to gain from this program?

4. Why do you feel it's important to be in good physical shape?

Handout: Follow-up

Distribute to the student after Lesson 12 (optional).

Answer the following questions in your own words.

1. What have you learned that is most important to you since you started boxing?

2. What do you like best about the boxing program?

3. If you could change anything in the boxing program, what would it be?

Sample Parents' Handout

Distribute to parents or guardians prior to starting the program. (optional)

Take a deep breath and relax. The fact that you are reading this means your child showed an interest in amateur boxing.

The good news is that amateur boxing is nothing like professional boxing. It is ranked seventy-first amongst amateur sports for injuries. It's not about knocking your opponent out. Each technically correct punch is worth a point. The focus is on scoring as many technically correct punches as possible without taking any risk to score one hard punch. A knockdown will not score any points, only punches that led up to it will score if they were thrown correctly. The bout is for three rounds, not ten or twelve like professional boxing. The boxers wear approved protective equipment such as headgear, mouthpiece, proper weight gloves, and groin protector. Physicals and weigh-ins are required prior to any competition. There are no weight discrepancies as in football.

It is my opinion that boxing is the most regulated and supervised amateur sport. There are no monetary gains for anyone.

The fitness level is higher then in other amateur sports. To that will come all the positive benefits, and at the same time boxing will educate the student with optimistic and constructive life skills. The habits developed through boxing will be influential in building other abilities and traits to be successful today and in the future. It will be with the person forever.

Some of the good qualities of the sport of boxing are motivation, confidence, self worth, discipline, goal setting, self-control, sports-manship, and character building. Many of these traits can be seen in top executives, and these qualities will take a person to the top.

From a parent's perspective, the positive release of energy (and juvenile frustration) is reason enough to be excited about the program, not to mention its aestheticism. Enjoy the path your child has chosen; it is an exciting one as well as rewarding. Nurture, guide and watch them grow.

Final Note to the Instructor/Coach

Now that you have given the student a solid foundation and under-
standing of boxing, they will need to add to it, while refining. Your
task will be to keep a close watch over them so they do not stray
from the fundamentals. While doing this you must keep them
motivated. Not all will need motivation, but most will. Encourage
their creativity and nourish it. In doing so, you will nourish your
own. Stay fresh keeping abreast of what's new, watch tapes (*Ringside* products has just about everyone you can imagine). If you have
access to the internet go online and check out *Boxinginsider.com* the
web-site will keep you up to date on the sport, *also* read books, one
of my favorite books is *Coaching Olympic Style Boxing* (a must read
for the coach). Go to as many fights as you can, visit gymnasiums
and watch boxing on television. Friday night fights (on *ESPN*) are a
great learning experience and Teddy Atlas & Max Killerman are
priceless.

Conclusion

Advanced routines/variations/additions

Continuing on to competition

Glossary

Additional Equipment required

Slip-cord

Advanced Routines and Variations

Upon completion, repeat the program from Lesson 1 with the following additions:

1. Begin sparring once a week, in addition to the two days of training per week. Incorporate free style at ¾ speed.

2. Incorporate movement into the bag workouts such as: circling, in and out, backpedaling, defensive movements, hitting on angles (hit & move, move & hit).

3. Incorporate additional drills during speed bag work from Lesson 8, such as the following:

    1. Double hits: strikes to the bag with both hands at the same time.

    2. Hooks, double and single 3-3.4-4, 3-4 or 4-3.

    3. Rhythms: 1,1-2,2 or 1,1,2 or 2,2. (Alternating combinations to increase hand-eye coordination).

    4. Trapping: trap the bag, not allowing it to fall; keep it pinned to the platform.

    5. Straight punches: box the speed bag as if it were a person. Throw a 1 or 1,1 or 1,1,1 or 1,2 or 1,2,3 or 1,2,1. The combinations are endless. Remember to incorporate footwork with head movement and angles.

4. Refer to *Ringside Products* countering video. There are some great charts to go along with it on counter punching which are more advanced then what I have put in this book. At this point you will be more inclined to perform them.

5. Work freestyle on the bags using the entire repertoire of offense and defense.

6. Increase the defensive countering drills to 2 opposing different punches. Example:

   Punches thrown: 5-6, counter with right/left palm block, throw 4-5. Or punched thrown: 1-1, counter with right parry-inside slip, throw 2.

7. Review techniques about drawing your opponent in. Example: by using fakes/feints.

8. Step in on punches number 1, 2, 3, and 5. Doing so will increase the power of the punch. Combining this with sitting on your punches will give you maximum power. An example of this is taking short step forward with your left foot, making sure your right foot is stationary and solid to the floor (not moving). Doing this transfers all your body weight and causes forward momentum to go into the punch. To sit on the punches simply drop your waist, hips and legs, as if you were sitting in a chair with your buttocks parallel to the floor

Continuing on to Competition

You can use all the preceding routines as a solid foundation, but you will need to add to it, especially for pre-competition. Use the list below as a starting guide for new topics that need to be addressed.

1. Nutrition: diet, weight and meal planning for optimal performance.

2. Fight strategy/analysis.

3. Rules of competition.

4. Interval training. An example is the variation to the long run (Advanced long run) in Lesson D

5. Advanced countering with movement. Example: punch thrown: 1, counter with 1-b, pivot & slide right, throw 4-b, 4, 3.

6. Train at least three to four days per week.

7. Begin using a slip-cord, also referred to as walking the rope. Example: tie a rope between two points and proceed to move forward and backward simulating throwing punches, at the same time slipping under the rope from side to side (left to right) working head movement.

8. Begin learning the art of infighting. Example: make a circle on the floor (6 x 6) and tie a rope between yourself and another boxer's waist so that you will not be able to separate more then three feet. Throw punches only to the body at first. Slowly increase to throwing full speed to the entire body and head. Make sure you are in full protective gear!

9. Begin learning to fight (throw punches) in between the opponent's punches with no set transition between offense and defense. This can be referred to as advanced countering.

Glossary

16 Oz: Weight of boxing gloves

Abs: Abdominal muscles

Ankle weights: Weights worn strapped around your calves varying in weight from 1 lb. to 5 lbs.

Box: Plyometric box. Dimensions are as follows: ranging in height from 6 to 24 inches. Top (landing surface) is 18 to 24 inches.

Chin-up bar: A bar of wood or steel suspended across a horizontal span above your head to propel yourself up and down.

Cones: Plastic cones ranging in height from 8 to 24 inches.

Countering: Hitting your opponent during or immediately after his/her attack.

Cutting off the ring: Refer to Lesson 14

Dip bar: A pair of tubular bars parallel to one another used to propel yourself up and down.

Dumbbell: Hand held weight.

Flinch: To draw back from something

Lats: Latissimus dorsi

Pecs: Pectoral muscle

Pivot and Slide: Refer to Lesson 3

Plyometric ball: Resembles a weighted basketball. Comes in varying weights.

Plyometric box: Refer to "Box"

Point: Shoulder out in front of your chin, standing vertical to your opponent (sideways).

Push-up handle: A handle is placed on the floor to elevate yourself six inches from floor for the purpose of getting lower during a push up provides for more of a stretch in the chest.

Quads: Quadriceps

Range fighting: Fighting from a distance

Reps: Repetitions (number of times you do something)

Roll Out: Side step to the left or right moving out of punching range

Roman chair: Also referred to as a "Hyperextension bench," it is a piece of equipment that enables you to do a reverse sit-up by securing your legs (holding down on your calves) while you lay on your abdomen/pelvis.

Slip-cord: A rope tied between two points about fifteen feet apart. The boxer U-slips while walking and throwing punches under the rope. When it is time to make a turn he pivots and slides left or right without breaking contact with the rope. The rope stays on the shoulder throughout the exercise.

Set: A consecutive series of repetitions

Stick and move: To throw a punch or punches and move out of the way immediately, before your opponent throws a counter punch.

Straps: Device resembling a sling that is secured to a chin-up bar, for the purpose of suspending yourself in mid-air without the use of your arm muscles to perform abdominal exercise.

Throw: Punch

Traps: Trapezoids

Weighted-neck strap: Headband going around the head that is weighted with sand (5 lbs.).

Wheel: A double wheel with handles on the sides on which you roll forward and backward on the floor with only your knees touching the floor.

CREDITS

Rafael Ayala is a kung-fu instructor and the owner of the Sarasota Shao-lin Academy (tiger crane method). He is the most dedicated person to the art I have ever met (He truly lives it.) I have learned a lot about myself from him (my true calling, to say the least). Peace.

Anthony Grasso is one of the finest photographers in the business, a true professional! His work speaks for itself.

John Garisto helped with editing/proofreading the script. It was a pleasure working with you, thanks.

Mark Malinowski is the publisher/creator of the international distributed interview feature the "*Biofile*". He also writes for seven different boxing publications, *BOXING DIGEST, WORLD BOXING, BOXING 2004 BOXING UPDATE, THE FIST AUSTRALIA, WORLD BOXING JAPAN AND BOXINGINSIDER.COM.* His enthusiastic ideas, encouragement, and friendship made the book possible. Thank you "Scoop". You can reach him through his web-site: thebiofile.com.

Derby Perez, you believed in me since the beginning and are a great source of my strength. Peace.

Mark Quartello, the book would not be possible without the "Life's Lessons" I have learned from you. They have helped make me the man and farther, I am today. Thank You Mark.

Harold Wilen, this business is like swimming in a sea of sharks and you have been the island! Thank you very much for the many hours of use of your gym and your friendship.

To all my Students, especially Kenny Blair. Kenny one day you will hold a championship title of your choosing. Without people like my students, this book would not be needed. I have learned as much from all of you as I feel I have taught you. Thanks.

CREDITS

Grant Boxing: thank you for your cooperation and use of your products. They truly are a quality product. I admire what your CO. has accomplished in such a short period of time, taking on giants in the industry. Grant Boxing can be found on the web at www.grantboxing.com

Index

About the Author

R. Michael Onello is a former amateur champion and owner of a boxing school in Sarasota Florida. He has over twenty-years experience in the sport of boxing and is currently a licensed professional boxing coach and trainer as well as an author with a diverse background in diet, nutrition and herbalogy. His opinions on the fight game are often quoted in national boxing magazines and on the Internet. In addition to instructing boxers in his home state of Florida, he has taught around the US and as far away as South America. He continues to actively expand his knowledge of boxing, attending the training camps of world champions and consulting with some of the top trainers in the business.

The author (R) with World Heavyweight Champion Lennox Lewis (C) and student Kenny Blair (L). (photo: Mark Malinowski)

Also Available from Turtle Press:

The Fighter's Body: An Owner's Manual
The Science of Takedowns, Throws and Grappling for Self-defense
Fighting Science
Martial Arts Instructor's Desk Reference
Guide to Martial Arts Injury Care and Prevention
Solo Training
Fighter's Fact Book
Conceptual Self-defense
Martial Arts After 40
Warrior Speed
The Martial Arts Training Diary
The Martial Arts Training Diary for Kids
TeachingMartial Arts
Combat Strategy
The Art of Harmony
Total MindBody Training
1,001 Ways to Motivate Yourself and Others
Ultimate Fitness through Martial Arts
Weight Training for Martial Artists
A Part of the Ribbon: A Time Travel Adventure
Herding the Ox
Neng Da: Super Punches
Taekwondo Kyorugi: Olympic Style Sparring
Martial Arts for Women
Parents' Guide to Martial Arts
Strike Like Lightning: Meditations on Nature
Everyday Warriors

For more information:
Turtle Press
PO Box 290206
Wethersfield CT 06129-206
1-800-77-TURTL
e-mail: sales@turtlepress.com

http://www.turtlepress.com

Boxing: The American Martial Art